The Art of Asking Questions

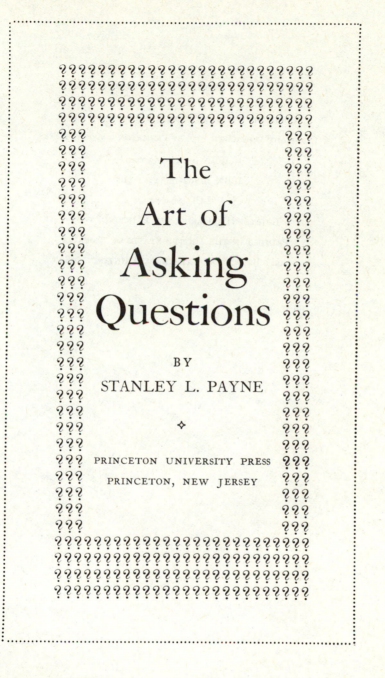

The
Art of
Asking
Questions

BY
STANLEY L. PAYNE

✦

PRINCETON UNIVERSITY PRESS
PRINCETON, NEW JERSEY

TO

Claude Robinson

WHO INSISTS THAT COMMUNICATION
IS OUR GREATEST PROBLEM

Foreword (1980)

THE PROLIFERATION of media-sponsored public opinion polls has made survey techniques and results familiar to many if not most Americans. The commercial television networks and many of the country's leading newspapers and magazines have set up their own polling operations—of widely varying degrees of sophistication and competence—and give extensive news coverage to these survey findings. Contributing to broad public awareness and acceptance of public opinion polls has been the unprecedented number of state political primaries and caucuses that will be conducted this year, each of which has been or will have been subjected to some form of public opinion research scrutiny.

For these reasons alone I feel it is particularly opportune that Princeton University Press has decided to issue *The Art of Asking Questions* in paperback.

In a careful rereading of this volume, I have found none of Stanley Payne's trenchant observations to be any less appropriate today than they were almost thirty years ago, when the book was written. Indeed, while great strides have been made in improved sampling design and technique—and electronic data processing has given us almost immediate access to the survey findings themselves—there has not been a comparable amount of progress in perfecting question or questionaire design.

From my perspective, there are at least three major factors contributing to this lack of progress.

1. The costs involved in collecting, processing, and interpreting survey data and disseminating the results have far outstripped inflation during the past thirty years. Since Stanley Payne arrived at many of his conclusions by experimenting with different question wordings by using the "split ballot" technique, and since this practice is both expensive and time-consuming, it is today more honored in the breech than in the observance.

2. The acceptance and growth of the survey research business and the increased dependence of the media and industry on information derived from marketing and opinion polls have spawned a demand for "instant results," often within a few hours after the interviewing has been completed. This climate of immediacy, in my opinion, does not lend itself to the kind of painstaking analysis and systematic inquiry that Payne so evidently followed as background for this book.

3. The enormous growth in the public opinion profession in the three decades that have elapsed since this book was written has inevitably drawn many people into the field who do not share the same degree of professionalism and motivation that was the hallmark of Payne and many of the pioneers of public opinion survey work in the 1930's and 1940's.

There is little doubt in my mind that in the future survey researchers must devote far more attention to question wording than they have in the past. When reputable survey organizations publish findings on behavior, attitudes, and opinions that vary widely, the validity of the whole survey procedure is challenged.

Payne underscores the importance of question wording by pointing out that a difference in wording can, on occasion, yield results that vary by 20 percent or more, whereas different sampling procedures rarely produce findings that vary by half this amount. Even sample size seldom makes so great a difference as that which comes from different questions seeking to assess the same attitudes and opinions.

For readers who simply want to ask better questions, for journalists, writers, and teachers, and especially for those professionals who are presently engaged in all aspects of survey research, *The Art of Asking Questions* should be indispensable reading. It needs to be read and reread by all of us.

GEORGE GALLUP

Princeton, N.J.

Foreword

ALTHOUGH a number of books have already appeared in the relatively new field of public opinion and market research, there is no book like this one. It is important and timely as well as unique. It deals with the warp and woof on which all surveys depend—the use of words.

"Spoken language," wrote Whitehead, "is merely a series of squeaks." And anyone who reads what Mr. Payne has written here will get a concrete understanding of what Whitehead meant when he said that "Language . . . is always ambiguous as to the exact proposition which it indicates."

There has been a long-standing and wide recognition of the care needed in asking the right question in the right way, as the author points out. But all too often this recognition seems to remain on the intellectual and verbal level of lip service with the importance of constructing the right question neglected in practice both in the survey operation itself and in the research conducted to improve methods. The apparent reasons for the relative neglect of the area Mr. Payne has probed reflect the temper of the times.

For one thing, those of us engaged in "research" like to think of ourselves as "scientists." We like to think that there are certain "rules" which we can discover and follow in order to be "objective." And we tend to think that if we can only quantify our material and manipulate it statistically, then, and only then, are we being "scientific." Hence, much of our research deals with technical problems of measurement.

But the author quite bluntly says he is dealing with an art, not a science, and the title of this book reflects, I think, a correct understanding of scientific procedure itself. For nearly any scientist whom we or history would label as "great" agrees that it is quite mythical to think of the scientist as being "objective." The scientist is involved in making personal value judgments at nearly every stage of his work— in the setting of his problem, the selection of the aspects of the problem which he feels are crucial and should be investigated, the selection of the method he will use for his investigation, as well as the interpretation of his results. Real scientific research of any kind is rooted in value judgments. The list of outstanding scientists in any field would show that these men and women were essentially great artists in the sense that they had the intuitive capacity to ask themselves the right questions in the right way at the right time.

The intuitive hunches or hypotheses which have given us giant strides in our understanding of nature or of human nature have seldom been created by following any rule of thumb or any one method. And especially in the area of inquiry with which the author deals here, the number of variables that must be implicitly taken into account are legion. They are also subtle and they defy quantification. They cannot be unwoven and analyzed independently for each depends on the others for its own existence and function. Survey questions tap an individual's motives, his expectancies, his unique experiences, his whole range of identifications and loyalties. In short, they are trying to discover certain aspects of what we might call an individual's assumptive world, a world which he himself has constructed during the course of life as he has attempted to work out a set of conditions within which he can satisfy the urges that characterize him as a human being.

Since the framing of the right question in the right way does involve so many subtle aspects, an investigator's intuitive ability to devise the right questions will be proportional to the number of cues and signposts he takes account of consciously and unconsciously as he goes about his task. The insights and cautions the author points out in the present volume should go far to increase the range of inclusiveness of the cues which investigators who study this volume can bring to bear in the process of question construction. Yet even if an investigator does test his question against the sample one hundred considerations the author cites at the end of the volume, he must remember that he is still being an artist, that he still has the intuitive value judgment to make of how to weigh and integrate these one hundred considerations in relation to the concrete situation he is trying to get at.

In addition to our bias of wanting to keep research "scientific" in an artificially restricted way, there may be another reason why no book like this has so far appeared in spite of the crucial nature of the problem. This is the tendency for those persons who reach high degrees of skill as practitioners to hesitate or neglect to try to put down in print some verbalization describing the skills they have attained. Many times such practitioners have little interest in doing this; usually they are too busy; some have no particular facility to generalize from rich backgrounds of experience. As a consequence, those of us who do not have the opportunity, the inclination, the ability, or the stamina to put ourselves in the position of participating in the actual occasions that constitute a certain area of life, may be forced to operate in a comparative darkness which we should like to have reduced.

In so far as an investigator is not constantly forced to test his assumptions as to what constitutes a good question in actual situations, he may tend to create in his mind, for reasons of expediency, an image of a non-existent "average" respondent. And he may do this even though, intellectually, he may realize fully that there is a long and devious route from the central office where questionnaires are designed on the basis of a certain amount of pretesting to the final reporting of the answers interviewers send in.

Mr. Payne is one of those rare individuals who has taken

time off to try to find out what this experience adds up to and how the art of asking questions may be described. A book as rich in insight as this could only have been written by someone who has had long and varied experience and who has sensed the difficulties encountered in real situations. The problems he raises and the answers he gives are derived directly from concreteness. And it is these problems derived from concrete experience that the academician or the investigator whose job confines him primarily to a desk are apt to be unaware of. Perhaps the author's major contribution is his own formulation of what questions to ask about asking questions.

While this book is written chiefly with the practical, everyday problems of question wording in mind, it is by no means confined in its usefulness to those people whose job it is to construct or to ask questions. For the problems the author raises and the illustrations and data he brings to bear on these problems pose a number of questions of theoretical interest for specialists in a variety of areas. The sociologist will see in Mr. Payne's material problems relating to concepts such as class, status, and social change; psychologists will see problems related to concepts such as frame of reference, ego involvement, and the attributes of opinion; semanticists will find documentation for many of their generalizations dealing with sources of misunderstanding as men try to communicate with one another.

The reader should be forewarned that the easy and light style of Mr. Payne's writing should not obscure the difficult and serious problems he writes about. The author has deliberately tried to write an interesting, highly readable book. I believe he has succeeded. And I believe that even the most experienced investigator, if he has a sense of humility at all, will learn a great deal from this little volume.

HADLEY CANTRIL

Princeton University
Princeton, N.J.

Preface

IN THE FIRST PLACE, this little book was not written by an expert in semantics, not even by a specialist in question wording. The author is just a general practitioner in research. Having made more than my share of mistakes in phrasing issues for public consumption and feeling the need for a book on the subject, I found that it was necessary to write it myself. In the process, my respect for the semanticist has increased beyond words. He is smart enough to use symbols to represent his ideas, but I have been so foolish as to try to use words in talking about words.

In the second place, this book is very limited in its subject matter. It discusses the wording of single questions almost exclusively. It hardly touches upon problems of question sequence or the overall matter of questionnaire design. It seemed difficult enough to deal with wording alone. Perhaps another book and another writer will cover these other subjects.

Third, the reader will be disappointed if he expects to find here a set of definite rules or explicit directions. The art of asking questions is not likely ever to be reduced to easy formulas. As it stands, this book consists of some observations of human behavior, a few principles of wording, many exceptions to these principles, several unexplained odd-ities, and numerous unsolved dilemmas. It is undoubtedly richer on the how-not-to side than on the how-to side. For want of a better description, it might be thought of as a collection of possible considerations for question wording.

Fourth, I happen to think that even a serious subject can be treated too seriously. Consequently, I have included some of the amusing and perhaps irrelevant ideas which occurred to me as I wrote. In other words, I have enjoyed writing this book. I hope you will enjoy reading it.

Last but not least, my apologies and thanks to all the people who graciously consented to read the original manuscript. I have not always acted on their suggestions, but I do appreciate their aid and counsel. Among those friends and colleagues whose criticisms have been especially stimulating are: Joseph Bevis, George Caldes, Frank Chokel, George Cole, Thomas Crawford, W. Phillips Davison, Richard Dittmer, Kendrick Few, Kenneth Fink, LeBaron Foster, Joseph Goeke, Joseph Hochstim, Arthur Holland, Roger Lloyd, Robert Mayer, Raymond Nasssimbene, Benjamin Phillips, Donald Rugg, Esther Schwartzstein, J. Stevens Stock, Knute Warren, and Albert Westefeld. My strongest plea for forgiveness and deepest appreciation go to Lucy Leigh, who so obligingly labored over every word with me.

STANLEY L. PAYNE

Contents

The Art of Asking Questions

1. Why concern yourself?

A PLEA FOR THE IMPORTANCE OF ASKING GOOD QUESTIONS

WHAT is the need for this first book on question wording? No one else has considered it necessary to devote a whole book to the subject. A chapter or two has always seemed enough before. Articles of several pages frequently appear in professional journals here and there. What more can a book do for question wording? If it all boils down to the familiar platitudes about using simple, understandable, bias-free, non-irritating wordings, all of us recognize these obvious requirements anyway. Why say more?

Oblivious of the obvious

One reason for elaborating on the subject is that all of us, from time to time, forget these requirements. Like some church-goers, we appear to worship the great truths only one day a week and to ignore them on working days. Or we remember a certain example, but fail to see how it applies to other situations. In combatting our very human frailty, a more provocative set of examples and a detailed list of points to consider may be more helpful than the isolated examples and the broad generalities which we now so often disregard.

The import IS important

Another reason for separate treatment is to help us realize how basic the phrasing of questions is to worthwhile research. As it is, we may look upon the few available examples of differences wrought by wording as mere freak occurrences. There is no danger of *our* making such weird mistakes, we think. Besides, if the question "works," it must be a good question.

By now, we should realize that the fact that something "works" does not mean that it works correctly. The *Literary Digest* poll seemed to "work" all right until 1936. The methods of subsequent election polls seemed to "work" all right until 1948. In both of these cases, attention has concentrated on sampling difficulties as causes of the wide margins of error. In the case of the *Digest* the faulty sample was no doubt the prime contributor to the error. At least one expert had predicted how and why this faulty sample would lead to error (1). In the more recent case, sampling is only one of the many possible causes, according to the Social Science Research Council committee (2).

Be that as it may, people—laymen and qualified experts alike—are impressed that sampling is an important feature of the survey method. Even if we agree that they are right, however, let us not forget that the Gallup Poll in 1948 overestimated the Dewey vote by *only* 4.4 percentage points, and the *Digest* poll in its 1936 prediction of the Landon vote was *only* 19 percentage points too high.

I use the word "only" advisedly because, as we shall see, survey differences resulting from changes in words or phrases sometimes amount to considerably more than a 19 point error! Perhaps, if we grant that by emphasizing the importance of sampling the election upsets have contributed to advances in sampling techniques, we should deplore the fact that nothing similar has happened to concentrate attention on the importance of question wording.

Tens versus tenths

At the present stage of development of the survey method, improvements in question wording and in other phases can contribute far more to accuracy than further improvements in sampling methods can. I don't mean that the sampling experts should stop seeking further improvements, trying to knock a few more tenths of a percent off the statistical error.

But, while they are laboring with tenths of a per cent, the rest of us are letting tens of per cents slip through our fingers. As Frederick Stephan of Princeton University has remarked, "It's like using a surgeon's scalpel in a butcher shop."

The experts said so

Even as far back as 1936, however, when the *Literary Digest* was riding to its fall, a group of experts called question wording the Number One problem. Howard T. Hovde asked a sample of researchers what they saw as the principal defects of commercial research (3). Here are their most frequently mentioned criticisms:

Improperly worded questionnaires	74%
Faulty interpretations	58
Inadequacy of samples	52
Improper statistical methods	44
Presentation of results without supporting data	41

Since three experts in every four pointed their fingers at question wording, it seems that the subject should have been worthy of concentrated attention. The specialists in statistics and sample theory certainly didn't let these expert opinions dampen their efforts. It's too bad that question worders weren't more stimulated by Hovde's report.

Samuel A. Stouffer and his collaborators in their recent monumental work on the American soldier (4) came to a similar conclusion: "To many who worked in the Research Branch it soon became evident that error or bias attributable to sampling and to methods of questionnaire administration were relatively small as compared with other types of variation—especially variation attributable to different ways of wording questions."

Jack-of-all-trades

Probably the reason that the question worder hasn't done more to advance his phase of research is that he just doesn't exist, at least not as a specialist. The statistician is the only one among us who has a specialty. All the rest of the work comes under the jurisdiction of a jack-of-all-trades. This man's job is to develop the questionnaire, pretest and revise it, have it printed, select, train, and supervise the interviewers, conduct the survey, analyze the results, write the report, and present the findings. His attention is necessarily divided. Question phrasing is but one part of the complex machinery which he must put together and operate. Small wonder that this all-around type of researcher has not had much time to formulate detailed statements on question wording.

Not special pleading

Having said that sample theory has moved ahead through specialization, I do not mean to imply that question wording needs also to be treated as a specialty. In actual practice, wording cannot be thought of as being in a vacuum apart from other phases of the survey method. It would be extremely naive to expect a single question to provide "some magic way of reducing a complex matter of people's attitudes, wishes, and aspirations to some simple wording which will not bias the returns." Most researchers will agree with Daniel Katz (5) that the solution usually requires "an integrated questionnaire which explores the problem comprehensively from many angles."

The fact that this book deals with the subject of question wording by itself and usually in terms of improving a single question does not mean that the other phases of the work can be slighted. The steel square is a useful tool to the carpenter and much can be said about its proper use without denying his need for jack-plane, saw, hammer, nails, and so forth. Several books are available on the use of the steel square. It is in much the same way that I advocate paying serious attention to question framing. For people who are also interested in the more general features of the question- naire technique, I might suggest Albert Blankenship's first book, *Consumer and Opinion Research* (6).

All types of surveys

The importance of wording is not restricted to any single type of survey. The mail questionnaire presents much the same problems of wording as the personal interview. The so-called "factual" survey is in need of careful wording just as the attitudinal or opinion survey is. Although opinion surveys present the greatest variety of examples, experience in factual or census-type enumerations also furnishes enough examples to show that facts as reported in answer to ques- tions are not always the facts that exist. We shall draw upon experience with all these types of surveys here, but most of the discussion will be based upon opinion surveys conducted by personal interview. First, then, let us look at some opinion questions.

Implied alternatives

Sometimes the questioner assumes that the negative side of the question is so obvious that it need not be stated. He may simply ask:

Do you think most manufacturing companies that lay off workers during slack periods could arrange things to avoid layoffs and give steady work right through the year?

> 63% said companies could avoid layoffs,
> 22% said they couldn't, and
> 15% had no opinion.

The alternative here seems to be so implicit in the question that it need not be stated. Either companies could avoid layoffs—or they couldn't. No other interpretation seems possible. But what happens when we take the trouble to state an alternative to another carefully matched cross section of respondents?

Do you think most manufacturing companies that lay off workers in slack periods could avoid layoffs and provide steady work right through the year, or do you think layoffs are unavoidable?

35% said companies could avoid layoffs,
41% said layoffs are unavoidable, and
24% expressed no choice.

So, a few words changed here and there and explicit statement of the other side of the picture results in a 28 per cent falling off from the affirmative side of this question!* This suggests the need for definite expression of the alternatives. Most of the discussion about alternatives, however, can be postponed to later chapters where we will not be so intent upon demonstrating the basic importance of wording.

Three little words

When we see the three words—*might, could* and *should*— together, we realize that they have somewhat different connotations. Yet when it comes to stating questions, we may sometimes use these words as synonyms. The trouble with this assumption is that the public actually does see distinctions among these words and changes its replies to fit. Here are the results of an experiment in which all things other than these words were kept equal. A casual reader might not detect the differences among these three questions:

Do you think anything should be done to make it easier for people to pay doctor or hospital bills?

---

* This example, as well as many others throughout these pages, came from the files of *The Public Opinion Index for Industry*, a service of Opinion Research Corporation, Princeton, N.J.

Do you think anything could be done to make it easier for people to pay doctor or hospital bills?

Do you think anything might be done to make it easier for people to pay doctor or hospital bills?

But enough respondents understand the distinctive feature of each connotation that significant differences show up in the replies of three matched samples of people: 82% said something *should* be done, 77% said something *could* be done, and 63% said something *might* be done. The two extremes, *should* and *might*, come out 19 per cent apart. This is the same amount by which the *Literary Digest* poll missed the 1936 election. Again we see that wording is as important as sampling, at least in opinion polls.

The issue at question

Question wording involves more than toying around with this word and that to see what may happen, however. It is more than a mere matter of manipulation of words to produce surprising illusions. The most critical need for attention to wording is to make sure that the particular issue which the questioner has in mind is the particular issue on which the respondent gives his answers.

If we refer again to the three questions using *might*, *could*, and *should*, we observe that they pose different issues. The *should* wording brings up the moral issue of need in the sense of, "It's a crying shame! Something *should* be done about it." The *could* wording poses the issue of possibility, "Yes, but *could* anything be done?" The *might* wording moves to the issue of probability, "Maybe it could, but it *might* or might *not* be done." The results show that more people see the moral need for an easier payment method than grant the possibility of doing anything about it and that even fewer people think such a method is likely to be put into practice. These are three distinct sets of basic content. Yet any one of them might inadvertently have been used alone to cover any or all of the three contents.

To assure that the intended issue is understood, then, is a fundamental function of question wording. A large share of our discussion will be given over to ways and means of reproducing in the minds of respondents the same issues that are in our thinking.

Census "facts"

Now, for some examples of the importance of question phrasing in factual surveys. The U.S. Bureau of the Census no doubt produces more facts than any other organization anywhere. Its experts consider question wording an important feature of securing this wealth of information. They know that such facts as the number of employed workers, the average number of bedrooms in homes, and even the size of the population itself are susceptible to different interpretation according to the skill used in devising the questioning techniques.

Baby counting

Would you believe that in the decennial Census there is danger of undercounting the population because some parents neglect to report their infant children? This very real problem arises not so much because of any lack of pride in the new offspring, but apparently because the parents are not yet used to thinking of the new little "it" as a person. Consequently, the question was asked at every dwelling: *Have we missed anyone away traveling? Babies? Lodgers? Other persons staying here who have no home anywhere else?* The enumerator was also instructed to "be sure to include . . . all children, even the very youngest." In addition, he received an extra 10 cents for each Infant Card, which was to be filled for every child born in January,

February, or March 1950. These precautions probably helped in the recording of thousands of infants who might otherwise have been overlooked (7).

Found: 1,400,000 workers

Take the problem of estimating the millions of persons at work in the nation, as done in the Monthly Report on the Labor Force of the Census Bureau. Gertrude Bancroft and Emmett Welch have explained how a change in the questioning technique affected these estimates (8). Prior to July 1945 a single question was used. It asked, *Was this person at work on a private or government job last week?* Beginning in that month, two questions were substituted. The first of these merely asked what the person's major activity was during the preceding week. If the major activity was something other than working, the enumerator then asked whether in addition the person did any work for pay or profit during that week.

The upshot of this change in questions was that in the trial when both versions were used, the new questioning showed an increase of 1,400,000 employed persons over the old wording. About half of these additional workers had worked 35 or more hours during the week under consideration!

Found: 500,000 unused bedrooms

This next example is more one of change of definition than of the wording of the actual question, but in factual surveys the two so often go hand-in-hand that they may well be taken together. During World War II the Census Bureau conducted hundreds of surveys for the National Housing Agency. Among these were some for the Homes Use Service, which was interested in inducing home occupants in critical areas of housing shortage to make rooms available to war workers. The delicate problem posed to the Census Bureau

[11]

was to determine how many bedrooms were not in use as sleeping rooms in these areas.

This required asking a representative sample of home dwellers how many bedrooms they had and how many they were using for sleeping. It was necessary to explain that for the purpose a bedroom was any room except the living room, dining room, kitchen or bath, which contained a bed or which with the addition of a bed could be used as a sleeping room. When it came to asking how many of these bedrooms were in use, it was necessary to emphasize use by the occupants for sleeping. Excluded from this use were guest rooms; bedrooms used only as studies, sewing rooms, storage rooms, or play-rooms; and bedrooms reserved for the use of absent members of the family such as students away at school.

Surveys in 83 critical areas showed a total of 500,000 bedrooms not in current use for sleeping. Only a sixth of these had previously been offered for rent. Publication of these results, area by area, helped greatly to spur room registrations (9).

This was a case, often duplicated in other surveys, where the respondent was asked to consider a situation in somewhat unfamiliar terms. That playroom or sewing room had never been used as a bedroom! Yet for this survey it was called a bedroom. This survey was different from many in that the researchers recognized that they were inverting normal thinking and went out of their way to define just what was wanted. In other studies we sometimes seem to forget that we are dealing with an unfamiliar situation or in unusual terms.

A whiff of ammonia

We can leave the Census type of enumeration to speak for a moment of the facts developed in marketing studies, such as surveys of consumer habits. The example we shall use is illustrative of what may happen when we phrase our questions with unfamiliar terms, or with familiar terms used in unfamiliar ways.

Recently a questionnaire on the subject of household disinfectants was mailed to a national sample of housewives. Now, it happens that almost every manufacturer of a disinfecting product is anxious that his particular product be accepted as a general household disinfectant. You can verify this by looking at the label on almost any bottle whether it was introduced to your home as an antiseptic, germicide, laundry bleach, or for other uses. It seemed entirely natural, therefore, that the questioning should be done in terms of "household disinfectants."

Despite the manufacturers' wishful thinking, however, housewives tend to think of such products in terms of their specific uses. Consequently, only 1 per cent of the respondents reported using ammonia among their "household disinfectants." This made it painfully obvious that the reference to household disinfectants did not conjure up the thought of household ammonia.

A later survey asked about "bottled disinfectants, antiseptics, and bleaches." In answer to such questions, 40 per cent of the housewives reported that they had ammonia on hand! It is probable, of course, that even more ammonia users would have come to light if direct questions had been asked about that particular type of product.

What about pre-testing?

Perhaps most of the examples mentioned so far could have been discovered by careful pre-testing of the questions before putting them in the final questionnaire. Yet, even these faulty questions might have "tested all right" if the tester was not looking for the particular difficulties we have mentioned. The broom-straw test of a cake may show whether it is baked enough and still not tell a thing about its sweetness. The proof is in the eating. In other words, the value of testing lies first in knowing the points for which to test. Knowledge of the considerations that go into the original wording is essential to good testing.

Wording and testing necessarily go hand in glove. To shift all the responsibility from one to the other would, like taking off the glove, let both hand and glove go cold. Furthermore, it should not be overlooked that pre-testing is far from being fully developed and that even the most elaborate pre-tests may be restricted to a few areas and only a few hundred cases. Many of the examples which will seem obvious as we refer to them here could not be demonstrated except by full-scale surveys. Even the 19 point difference we have seen between *should* and *might* requires relatively large matching samples for demonstration and could not be expected to show up in a small-scale pre-test.

A critical reading of a questionnaire has been known to point out more problems than were detected in an earlier testing. One reason for this is that great limitations are placed on the tester; he usually cannot spend more than an hour in a single interview even with a long questionnaire. The experienced person who is working on the same question-naire in the office, on the other hand, can consider all angles and take as long as necessary in perfecting each phrase.

An alternative suggestion to leaving the problems to the testing is to take as much as we can into account in the original drafting. Pre-testing can accomplish much more if the questions already measure up to certain laboratory re-quirements and if certain possible problems are made the specific objectives of the pre-test. Incidentally, one of the pre-tester's most useful devices is the follow-up question: *What do you mean by that?*

Summing up

We now have exposed the importance of question wording in several lights. We see that it is too easily overlooked, that it has lacked the impetus to be gained from a major disaster such as the prodding given to sampling by the *Literary Digest* failure, but that it sometimes produces differences in results even greater than the error in that unfortunate poll. We note that wording can both benefit from and contribute to pre-testing. We see that wording presents problems in factual surveys as well as in opinion surveys. And we recognize that wording is more than a game like anagrams or acrostics—that it has the serious object of making certain that our meanings are understood.

The big shots

If after all this argument any doubt still remains about the importance of question wording in the survey method, here is one more demonstration. Let us sit in on any of the score or so questionnaire discussions that are in session this very minute and that may continue all day, or all week for that matter. Here we may see association executives, heads of government bureaus, corporation presidents, advertising geniuses, public relations advisers, and research consultants —all cudgeling their brains over how to ask Mrs. Zilch which umsquitch she likes best.

Besides showing how universally interesting is the subject of asking questions and that even important people think it important, an observer could learn many other things from such a conference. One of these provides an interesting commentary on the stage of development of question wording: No one in such conferences has a corner on all the good ideas that may go into a satisfactory question. The confessed amateur seems to come up with acceptable suggestions almost as often as the professed expert does. So all of us can take heart that we have an open field in which to try out our own ideas.

2. May we presume?

IF ALL the problems of question wording could be traced to a single source, their common origin would probably prove to be in taking too much for granted. We questioners assume that people know what we are talking about. We assume that they have some basis for testimony. We assume that they understand our questions. We assume that their answers are in the frame of reference we intend.

Frequently our assumptions are not warranted. Respondents may never before have heard of the subject. They may confuse it with something else. They may have only vague ideas about it and no means for forming judgments. Even if they know the subject, they may misunderstand the question or answer it in some unexpected sense.

As question worders we need to develop a critical attitude toward our own questions. We must check the tendency to accept the first wording that makes sense to us. We must subordinate any pride of authorship to this critical attitude and should try to substitute clarity for cleverness. Every objection that may be raised about the phrasing should be carefully considered, because that problem may occur many times over in the full-scale survey. If even a single test interview or comment from one of our associates implies any fault in the question, that fault should not be passed over. How many people in the final survey will stumble over the same obstacle?

The tendency to take things for granted is not easy to correct, simply because it is such a common characteristic of us all. It is a subtle fault, committed most, of course, when we are least aware of it. For this reason, some conscious safeguard is needed—self-discipline to stop and ask ourselves with each question, "Now, just what is being taken for granted here?" In a sense this whole book deals with the problem, but for sake of emphasis this one chapter brings out some glaring and perhaps surprising examples.

A pertinent example

With straight faces we might start our interviews among the general public by asking, *Which do you prefer, dichotomous or open questions?* We might be surprised at the proportion of people who would soberly express a choice. Their selections obviously would not be meaningful in the desired sense. Yet, it would be incorrect to assume that their answers were entirely meaningless or haphazard. People might vaguely think that they understood us but not knowing the first term might choose the second in high proportions. And in passing, we might forecast that repeated experiments with the same question would probably give closely duplicating results. Stability of replies is no test of a meaningful question. The more meaningless a question is, the more likely it is to produce consistent percentages when repeated.

The main point of the example is that laymen's answers to the question in this form could not be accepted as guidance in a technical dispute between advocates of the two types of questions. Essentially, this same mistake, usually in better disguise, is made again and again on matters or in words for which the public has no basis for testimony. The fact that we get answers to such questions is no proof of the pudding. It may only indicate that people like to testify and that they don't want to appear to misunderstand what they think must be a straightforward question.

Trick questions

We can sometimes readily recognize that answers are not very meaningful as in some trick questions reported by Sam

Gill (10). By asking without elaboration about an entirely fictitious "Metallic Metals Act" he got 70 per cent of the people to make judgments about it, such as whether it should be enacted nationally or left to the states. He got substantial proportions also to approve of incest! There is little danger of taking seriously either these results or those mentioned earlier on dichotomous questions. The moral is plain, however, that widespread knowledge of similar subjects should not be taken for granted.

Admissions of ignorance

In Gallup Poll questions, 45 per cent of the public said they did not know what a "lobbyist in Washington" is, 41 per cent said they did not know what the phrase "socialized medicine" means, 46 per cent could not describe what a "filibuster" is, and 88 per cent either said they didn't know or gave incorrect descriptions of "jurisdictional strike" (11).

Unless people are asked directly about their knowledge of terms like these, they are not inclined to mention that they don't understand them. Knowledge questions usually bring forth more "Don't knows" than do opinion questions on the same issues.

In an opinion question about watered stock, some 6 per cent of the public volunteered that they did not understand the term. In one on monopoly, 10 per cent confessed ignorance. These small proportions who freely stated their lack of familiarity furnish only minimum indications that other people may have given opinion answers with no knowledge or only vague notions of these terms.

These last few illustrations come from personal interviews. Lack of knowledge is probably just as important in mail questionnaires, but in these unfamiliarity may be obscured in two ways—by failure of the uninformed to return the questionnaire or by their opportunity to discuss the subject or to refer to it in dictionaries and other sources.

Either of these possibilities may make the mail returns un-representative as far as indicating the extent of general knowledge is concerned.

Profits

Or take the subject of profits (not "prophets," as a few respondents have understood the term). Here is the keystone of our economy. Surely the public should understand the function of profits and have some reasonable idea of returns on invested capital. Yet the accountant who assumes that his definition of profit is universally accepted has a shock coming. People variously think of profit in terms of gross margin, mark-up, volume of business, executive salaries, hidden profits, and so on. They may think that profits are high because the Vanderbilts own an interest in the company, or because the company gives worker benefits, or because it sells its products by the gross, or for many other reasons.

Scores of examples could be given of the misunderstanding of profits but here is a very illuminating one:

When you speak of profits, are you thinking of profit on the amount of sales, on the amount of money invested in the business, on year-end inventory, or what?

Profit on sales	22%
Profit on investment	18
Profit on inventory	14
Profit on other bases	10
Don't know	37

More than a third of the public in this survey admitted that they had no particular concept of profits in mind. More revealing, however, is the result showing that almost as many said they thought of a year-end inventory base as of the investment base! If we take this 14 per cent as an index of guessing, and discount the first two answers each by this amount, we can count on only 8 per cent who really meant profit on sales and 4 per cent who really meant profit on investment. In other words, if this line of reasoning were not itself so questionable, only 12 per cent of these people could be assumed to understand the accountant's method of figuring profit.

How ignorant!

Do all of these examples add up to the conclusion that most of the public is ignorant? Only in the sense that the city boy thinks the country boy is ignorant, and vice versa. The specialist may lose sight of the fact that others have no need for his jargon. He may think that, because his associates and his technical books use the same lingo, his brand of gobbledygook should be universal. But what does he himself know of the terminology in some other field beyond his own? Probably not any more than others among the uninitiated do.

In any case, it is useless to weep about how ignorant other people may be.

Nor do these examples reflect upon the public's native intelligence. People may have entirely reasonable attitudes about watered stock when they know that they are talking about finance instead of cattle. They may even be able to distinguish good and bad monopolies when the term is clarified. They can make judgments that profits are too high, too low, or reasonable without accepting the accountant's definition. They may be able to choose between two-way and free-answer questions if the issue is made clear to them.

Our job

This is one of the jobs we question worders have to do— to make these concepts understandable so that respondents may know whereof they speak. Nothing said here is meant to discourage us, but only to increase our awareness that we cannot say like Humpty-Dumpty, "When I use a word, it means what I choose it to mean." As question worders we must make sure that our meaning is comprehended by others.

Skillful questioning can obtain meaningful answers on attitudes surrounding such subjects as we have been discussing. But it is all-important to realize that the disclosure of lack of knowledge and of misinformation is basic to the understanding of these attitudes. One method of bringing these things to light is the filter approach: *Have you ever heard of such-and-such?* followed by *What would you say such-and-such is?* or *What examples can you give me of such-and-such?* Then, it may be found necessary to explain the subject before proceeding to ask further questions about it.

Wheat and chaff

The problem of taking too much for granted becomes more confounded as we approach subjects where one large part of the public speaks in the intended frame of reference, but another large part does not. The chaff that is mixed in with the wheat may not be detected by common measures. Erroneous conclusions may be reached in such cases.

For example, better educated people might appear to desire more "government ownership" of local utilities than the less well educated do. This might happen simply because the better educated include municipal ownership in their thinking of "government ownership," while the others tend to think only of ownership by the federal government. In other words, what on the surface appears to be a difference in political motivation related to education may instead be only a difference in interpretation of a word. If we should ask both groups about "federal ownership" or about "municipal ownership," quite the reverse of the original finding might result—the better educated might prove to have less desire

[21]

for either form of government ownership than the less well educated.

Whose zoo?

It can happen that different people will read directly opposite meanings into the same words. Let us imagine a community where feeling runs very high on a proposed referendum to sell the city zoo to a meat packer for use as a slaughter house. Then we ask the citizens, *Do you think that the sale of the zoo to the meat packer should go through, or not?* Both those who answer "No" and those who answer "Yes" could mean the same thing. Those saying "No" would probably mean that the zoo should not be sold, while those saying "Yes" might mean that the sale should "fall through."

$50 or $51

The researcher can even be tripped up by accepting factual replies to a perfectly understood question. I recall a situation during the war when the Census Bureau was conducting surveys of rental changes for the Office of Price Administration. The analysts were plagued by what appeared to be a number of small changes in reported monthly rents. These rents would move up or down without apparent rhyme or reason. The rent of a particular dwelling one month might be reported at $51.00 and the next month at $50.00.

Ordinarily, small differences like this would not be important, but since the purpose of the surveys was to determine the number of changes in rent and the average amount of change, these differences did assume considerable importance.

The explanation for the small changes was simple enough when discovered. It was traceable to tenants who paid their rent weekly instead of monthly. This had been anticipated and the interviewers had been given a simple conversion table which multiplied the weekly figure by 4 1/3 to arrive at an average monthly figure.

[22]

The trouble was that a tenant paying $12 a week might report it that way, making it $51 a month, or might do a rough rounding himself and report that his rent was "$50 a month." When he reported it one way in one survey and the other way in the next one, a fictitious rental change of $1 was deduced from the two figures. Of course, once this situation was discovered it was easily remedied by having the interviewers question the very small differences reported to them. In effect it amounted simply to asking whether the rent was paid weekly or monthly.

Minimizing DK's

The worth of questions is sometimes judged by the proportion of "Don't know" (DK) and "No opinion" replies. If only a few respondents hesitate to answer the question, it is ruled ipso facto a "good" question. Pre-testers may report that the question "works all right."

This criterion of high response is useful, but should not be followed blindly. Our hypothetical question about the zoo might command high response, but surely no one would want to defend it as a good question. A high response, then, may be obtained with a poor question.

With some questions a high response is not desirable and should not be expected. If most respondents have no basis for opinions but in effect would have to flip coins mentally for their answers, it would be better if their answers were not recorded. Forcing a choice where none exists is not realistic.

Another case where most people will not readily express an opinion is when they are asked to censure somebody, a company, or an industry. Surveys repeatedly show that while respondents are relatively free with their praise, they are loath to criticize. When asked which local company has the poorest working conditions, the weakest management, and so on, usually anywhere from 50 per cent to 90 per cent will not name names. This makes the minority responses all the more meaningful because they represent very sharp criticisms. It does not mean that the question is not good, although some attention to a milder wording of a negative question may help to produce more replies.

What I mean here in essence is that trying for a high response is in itself taking for granted that the high response is desirable, when sometimes it may not be.

Beware the expert

I have already hinted that the specialist in the subject matter which the survey is investigating may not be an expert in judging what the public knows about it. Helpful though his guidance may be in acquainting the researcher with the subject, his ideas can be harmful when he sets himself up as a prognosticator of public opinion. His pronouncements in this field need to be taken with more than a grain of salt, especially since the object of the survey is to provide him useful information. I might also add parenthetically that it is necessary to beware of the "specialist" among respondents. It might be assumed that a working man, or an industrialist, or a farmer would be able to predict more exactly how his group is going to behave than someone outside the group. This is not always the case, however. A group investigating political behavior in Elmira, New York, prior to the 1948 election found that the tendency of respondents "is to pull the group whose vote is being estimated in the direction of their own vote intention" (12).

This is perhaps being too critical of the specialist, however. What does sometimes happen is that a thing he takes for granted is not questioned by the researcher, who should be on guard against accepting such assumptions. Usually, if the researcher points out the possible dangers in the assumption, the specialist is willing at least to have it subjected to trial. A case in point was the manufacturer's assumption that housewives saw eye-to-eye with him on "household disinfectants." When told that this was only an assumption, he readily agreed to another wording.

Many other examples are available to show how the uncritical researcher can go wrong by blindly following the specialist's ideas. In one survey where a sample of all workers in an industrial city were to be interviewed in their homes, it was essential to report separately the attitudes of employees of four large manufacturing companies, A, B, C, and D. Of these, one was a parent company with several local subsidiaries having widely different company names. The personnel manager of the parent company (Company C) thought that the workers in the subsidiaries would know their connection with Company C because, for one thing, they were paid on Company C's checks. Nevertheless, when these very workers were asked, *By the way, do you happen to work for any of the companies on this list (A, B, C, D)?* many of them said "No." As far as they were concerned, they worked only for the subsidiary company and had nothing to do with the parent company.

A group of bankers wanted the public's appraisal of trust department services. Instead of asking directly what people thought of trust departments, however, the research agency suggested asking, *Would you tell me what you think the trust department of a bank does?* More than half of the respondents said they did not know, while some others thought the department was interested in loans, investigating to see whether a borrower could be "trusted," etc. Only a third gave answers that indicated correct information (13). This result meant that the banks needed first to acquaint people with the activities of the trust department before hoping to gain wide appreciation of it.

"This case is different"

An answer the specialist in subject matter may be inclined

to make is, "Yes, but this case is different. Look at all the publicity it has received." Or, "Our workers are different. They are kept up-to-date on such matters."

We researchers could become rich just by taking bets against such assumptions. One railroad thought that its workers would have far greater knowledge than railroaders nationally. But separate analysis as reported in *Railway Age* magazine (14) showed that only on two or three items were the comparisons favorable to the individual railroad. "On most questions, however, and on the average of all questions, the closeness of correlation between the opinions of the employees of this one railroad and those of employees as a whole is positively astonishing."

Differences between the national results of a public opinion survey for the American Petroleum Institute and the results in a single state where one company was thought to have made much greater progress than the rest of the industry averaged only about 3 per cent.

Who? Why? When? Where? How?

Another kind of expert of whom the researcher must be wary is himself. All along we will be discussing the need for making the issue clear to respondents. Even before that stage is reached, however, we must be sure that we understand the issue ourselves. Believe me, this is not an unnecessary admonishment! Many of the problems of question wording result from our going off half-cocked. Once the issue is posed in even the vaguest terms, we start trying to put it in words that are understandable to the public.

If we did but realize it, the first half of the battle consists of putting the issue in a form that we can understand ourselves. We need first and foremost to define the issue precisely, regardless of the general understandability of the words. The news reporter has his stock questions to ask himself about each item: Who? Why? When? Where?

How? We can well ask these same questions of ourselves for each issue we intend to pose. Another way of putting it is: "What conditions are we assuming in this issue?"

Let me illustrate without much further elaboration at this point. Here is an issue or question which we will come back to later:

Should our country be more active in world affairs?

This issue sounds like a good question for debate, but if you start asking the reporter's five questions about it, you will soon see that it is virtually meaningless.

You may have been a little surprised to read the earlier statement, "We need first and foremost to define the issue precisely, regardless of the general understandability of the words." That is exactly what I mean to say, however. If it will help to make the issue understandable to ourselves we should use the most precise terms possible even though they may not be widely understood. After we are sure that the issue is fully defined and that its limits are set to our satisfaction, then we can begin to translate it into simple words for public consumption.

In Chapter 13 we will go through this procedure of carefully defining an issue before starting to put it in everyday language.

Even simple words

Most of our earlier examples of taking too much for granted have involved the use of uncommon terms or complicated concepts—dichotomous, household disinfectant, Metallic Metals Act, profits, government ownership, trust department. Yet, the simple words of everyday usage may have the same pitfall of being taken too much for granted. A few illustrations will show how easy it is to fall into the trap.

One might expect that anyone who had just attended a Patents Exposition would reply affirmatively to this question: *Have you heard or read anything about patents lately?* Yet in an actual survey only half of the people who later in the interviews said that they had attended the Exposition said "Yes" to this question. Apparently, the "heard or read" phrase, as all-inclusive as it was meant to be, did not bring to mind what had been seen at the Exposition. People may not think of a display as being "read" even though it has a printed message.

In repeated surveys for the electric industry, only 3 people say that "rates" have come down in the past 15 or 20 years for every 4 who say that the average family gets "more electricity for its money today." From this and other evidence it appears that some people confuse the total amount of the electric bill with the kilowatt hour rate.

International pollsters, who must translate questions from one language to another, have particular difficulty in ensuring that the same word will have the same meaning to all respondents. Eric Stern reports, for instance, that in some countries of Europe the expression "washing machine" refers to the same implement we refer to in the United States. In at least one country, however, the term refers to a hand-turned agitator which fits over the top of a wash tub. To his amazement this researcher found that in that country the number of respondents who reported owning a "washing machine" was far higher than any other (15).

Commonplace errors

It goes without saying that the commonplace things of our daily existence are the ones we take most for granted. Most of us ignore much of the detail that surrounds our everyday lives. Yet the details that one man overlooks may be another man's livelihood. The calendar manufacturer assumes that I know whether the calendar over my desk shows a sailing vessel or a hunting scene. But caught away from the room, I may have to guess about it. And despite a sometimes faulty memory, my answer may come with considerable conviction.

The researcher can go astray by assuming that people are more aware of the commonplace than they actually are. The phenomenon of unobservance confronts us on every side. Its result is that answers come not in terms of the facts as they exist but in terms of what the respondent thinks the facts ought to be. When we rely on the faulty memory of a cross section of people, the popular calendar designs, brands of beer, and breakfast foods appear even more popular than they are.

If we require the real facts, an actual inventory is the surest means of getting them, according to the maxim that "one peek is worth a hundred guesses." The recall through memory does have valid uses, however. The point to keep in mind here is that recall may differ from fact, and therefore should not be taken as fact.

To amplify, here are a few examples of the kinds of detail that people frequently overlook:

Many people do not know the name of the company that makes their favorite breakfast food. Many men cannot tell the brand of shirt they are wearing now or the color of the tie they wore yesterday. Consumers are frequently at a loss to say whether their electricity comes from water power or steam generators and whether their gas stove is using manufactured or natural gas.

Waiters frequently find that people have forgotten what items they have just ordered. Salesladies will tell you that husbands don't know their wives' fundamental measurements. For that matter, they may not know their own glove sizes. Some people cannot give the cities of their parents' birth. Busy executives may know everybody's telephone extension but their own. Auto license numbers are often casualties of memory.

Few people are confused as to the parent company of the Chevrolet but many assign the Dodge to the wrong company.

More people still think of Standard Oil as a single national concern than realize that it was split into several independent companies many years ago—in 1911, to be exact. Sizable fractions think that their business-managed local utilities are owned by the city or state simply because the city or state name is included in their titles. Many brand names, like Kodak are sometimes thought of as generic terms rather than names of brands. Not many people can say which of the leading brands of watches are Swiss and which are American in manufacture.

Employees often do not know the titles of their own jobs. They can't enumerate all the automatic deductions taken from their pay. They don't always realize that their employer in effect has to match their Social Security payments. They don't recall their company's profit even though they read about it in the house organ.

An exercise

If we could keep these limitations in mind, we would not be so likely to slip into so many ready assumptions in wording questions. We would cock a wary eye at terms like competition, regulation, worker productivity, jurisdictional dispute, expenditure, unemployment, prohibition, commercials, private company, stockholder, nuclear fission, juke box, acne, detergent, TVA, P.M., tariff, dentifrice, excise tax, and annual wage.

Here is a simple exercise which may help you to remember how little you can take for granted. By demonstrating to your own satisfaction that people do not know grade school facts and have difficulty remembering important recent or current events, you will see why some questions may catch them flat-footed—even if they are logical thinkers.

Just ask some of your best friends as many of the following questions as you think will not endanger your friendships. Don't purposely seek out uninformed people. The demonstration will work practically as well with the intelligentsia. Try to answer all of these questions yourself for that matter:

What color is the complement of blue?
How do you spell Mabel?
What is the cube of 2?
Name the capital of Missouri.
Name our five largest cities.

Name a defeated vice-presidential candidate in the most recent national election.

Who are the U.S. Senators from this state?
What date is Columbus Day?
Without counting them, how many keys are on your key ring?
Again without counting, how many teeth do you have?

3. Who left it open?

A DESCRIPTION OF THE FREE-ANSWER QUESTION AND ITS DEMERITS

Many researchers feel very strongly about which type of question gives the most useful information. Some go so far as to take an almost proprietary interest in seeing that a particular type is used in every possible application. One school of thought contends that the free-answer type, to be discussed in this chapter, provides the most valid and un-influenced results. Another school maintains that the two-way choice comes closest to the common decisions we have to make in everyday life. Yet another group asserts the superiority of the multiple-choice question, because it allows for gradations of feeling or for expressions of a variety of alternatives.

Everybody's right

Of course, all of these schools of thought are correct depending upon the nature of the problem at hand. And while different persons may sometimes use directly opposite approaches to the same problem, most questioners do on occasion use more than one type of question. Most questionnaires include a variety of types. Occasionally, two types will even be combined in a single question as, *Do you think this or that, or what?*, a combination of two-way and free-answer. The Gallup Poll has devised a "Quintamensional Design" in which any issue is approached through five different paths before it is considered to be thoroughly explored (16). We shall come back to this design in chapter six after the various types of questions have been individually discussed.

We see that the advocates of the different types do not

hold out for exclusive use of a single approach even though they may have strong preferences. This is as it should be. It will always be too early to settle upon any one way of doing research. Particularly in this infant stage of the survey method, we do not want to find our young prodigy already suffering from hardening of the arteries.

The pros and cons of the three major types of question are many, so that it becomes necessary to examine each type at some length before getting into the details of wording. This general subject has been discussed briefly by Hadley Cantril and Donald Rugg in the former's book, *Gauging Public Opinion* (17). We shall devote several chapters to question types here.

Whatcha know, Joe?

In ordinary conversation, we may introduce a topic by asking, *What do you think about such and such?* This is a good example of the free-answer or open question. It may evoke an astonishing array of replies. So much so that we sometimes think it necessary to interrupt the answer by amplifying further: *I mean, what do you think about it in these terms?* Or our friend may anticipate by asking, *How do you mean that?* All three of these questions are free-answer questions because they leave the respondent free to offer any idea or ideas he may think of. He is not asked to make his answer conform to one of several ideas which are already outlined for him. His answers are free, open, unlimited. The free-answer question sets no definite alternatives and the respondent answers it in his own words. Interviewers are usually instructed to record the answers verbatim.

As simple as all this sounds, it is nevertheless possible to distinguish many basic varieties of free-answer questions. They range from the wide-open variety to what might be thought of as the slot variety, in which check boxes are provided for recording the answers even though these specific ideas are not suggested to the respondent.

An example of this last type would be, *How many people are there in your family living at this address?* While no answers are suggested, the thoughts of respondents are here directed into very definite channels, and check boxes should be provided for recording the numbers they are likely to give.

But let us start with the most wide-open varieties first:

Opener questions

Accepted theory indicates that it is usually best to proceed from the general to the specific. Consequently, "opener" or introductory questions tend to be of the most general free-answer type. They serve to lead into the subject, to elicit non-directed, unstructured replies, and to provide the background for interpreting the more detailed and specific questions that may be asked later in the questionnaire. They are non-directive except in so far as they indicate the general nature of the subject to be discussed. Of course, they vary in the degree of the direction thus given. A number of introductory questions may appear in a single questionnaire as the conversation moves from one topic to another. For example, in a community relations survey:

When you think of the three or four leading manufacturing companies here, which ones come to mind?

If a friend of yours who knew almost nothing about Beelzebub, Incorporated, asked you to describe the company, what would you tell him?

From a survey for the oil industry:

What kinds of activities and businesses do you think of as being included in the oil industry?

What is your idea of how retail gasoline and oil prices are decided?

What do you think happens to the money that is collected in gasoline taxes?

From a wartime survey among farmers:

What would you say have been your main difficulties in farming during the past year?

How did those difficulties affect your farm production?

What are some of the shortages that have bothered you most?

As you look forward to your farming this next year, what in the line of supplies or equipment is causing you the most concern?

In consumer market studies:

What's your reaction to this product, just from seeing it and smelling it?

When I mention the term "dextrose," what comes to your mind?

What does good quality in an alarm clock mean to you?

What things in particular would you look for in buying a toothbrush?

How did you go about buying your last pair of shoes?

What are the first things you look for in a bathing suit?

From various other surveys:

If you had a half hour to talk to the president of your company today, what things would you most want to talk to him about?

If a friend of yours asked you, "What is the New York Stock Exchange?", what would you tell him?

What do you think of when you hear the term "advertising"?

What are some of the big problems you'll probably face in running this business after the war?

What are your three favorite radio programs?

What one thing about the Breeze Wiper Company would you say it is best known for?

Will you tell me for whom you think this survey is being made?

Suggestions

Another kind of free-answer question, which may be even more wide-open than the introductory type, simply asks for suggestions. The variety of recommendations is limited only by the experience of respondents with the subject, their ingenuity, and their articulateness. It sometimes happens that as many as 90 per cent of interviewees will have suggestions to make. Many of these thoughts, of course, may not be feasible, but the usable ideas that do emerge are often very valuable.

What could the company do to build better relations with the public?

What conditions do you feel could be improved in this plant?

What more could they do for their workers?

At what time of day would you want your milk delivered?

Is there anything about Eentsie-Teentsie Breakfast Flakes that you don't like or think could be improved?

What particular facts do you think ought to be in a report like that?

If this type of survey is repeated, what other questions would you like to see added?

Follow-up questions

Sometimes further elaboration is needed as an aid to understanding the answers to a question. Follow-up questions like these below may be used after either free-answer or choice questions:

Would you tell me just how you feel about that?

What was the result?

In what way?

What was it you heard?

[36]

Would you mind telling me what you know about it?
Can you give me any examples of its progressiveness?
What did you hear or read that was unfavorable?
In what ways do you think you'd be affected?

Reason-why

The reason-why question is probably the most common type of free-answer question. It usually follows a choice question, and in its simplest form uses only one word, *Why?*

It cannot always be asked of everybody but may have to be confined to those who have made choices on the preceding question. If a person refuses to choose between the alternatives offered, for example, it would make little sense then to ask him, *Why do you choose that one?* Sometimes it is asked only of those who signify one particular choice. In other words, it is usually an "exclusion" type question, by which we mean one asked only of certain respondents.

Constant repetition of the one-word query *Why?* throughout an interview may become tiresome, border on impertinence, and stifle responses. Consequently, many variations of this question have been developed, but it is readily seen that they all boil down to the same idea. They do vary in the degree to which they direct respondents' thinking however:

Why particularly?
Why do you say that?
Why would you say that?
Why do you feel that way?
Why would you vote this way?
Why do you think that is so?
Why pick that one?
Why do you name that one?
Why do you prefer that one?
Why did you select that make instead of another?
Why do you say the public benefits?

[37]

Why do you suppose that company pays lower wages than the others do?

Why don't you belong to the co-op any more?

Why did you decide not to use it?

I wonder why you didn't receive it?

I'm interested in your reason for that.

What makes you say that?

What would you say are the reasons?

What do you think have been the main reasons for this?

What do you object to?

What things about that company cause you to think well of it?

What things do you think would be gained by government ownership?

What were your particular reasons for choosing this store instead of some other one?

What caused you to change your mind?

What indications do you go by?

How does that work out?

How did you happen to buy that brand?

How do you think that will come about?

How do you happen to know most about that company?

Paul F. Lazarsfeld found that the word "Why" could refer to one of a number of aspects of a situation (18). When asked why he bought a product, for instance, a respondent may reply in terms of a characteristic of the product, or he may explain that he just happened to see it on the shelf, or he may say that he was about to go on a trip and needed a supply of a product of that sort. It is important that the question-worder have a clear picture in his own mind to the type of answer he wants when he asks "Why?"

Argument type

The argument variety of free-answer question is closely akin to the reason-why variety. One distinction is that in the argument question we solicit ideas from all respondents regardless of which side they take on the issue. That is, arguments both for and against a given stand are asked of the same respondent rather than requesting only his own reasons for his own particular stand. It can be very revealing to learn which arguments the proponents of a given issue will admit as being the best arguments of its opponents, and vice versa. Sometimes we ask the argument question without having the respondent commit himself on one side or the other, however.

Argument questions, then, usually come in pairs and tend to be less personalized than the reason-why questions. The respondent testifying on the other side of the fence is not speaking for himself but for the opposition.

Can you tell me any of the arguments people make for prohibition?

Can you tell me any of the arguments people make against prohibition?

What do you think would be gained by dealer licensing?
What do you think would be lost by dealer licensing?

What things would you say are good about a library as a place to work?
What things are not so good?

What do you like best about your job—what are its good points?
What do you like least about your job?

What things do you like about every-other-day milk delivery?
What criticisms have you heard of the every-other-day plan?

What special advantages do you think small (large) businesses have in competing with large (small) ones?

What things about your alarm clock do you like particularly?

What things about your alarm clock do you dislike?

What do you think are the main reasons people join cooperatives?

We've talked about the advantages of co-ops—can you tell me some of the disadvantages?

What do you like about the information they give?
What don't you like about it?

In what ways would you say it is good?
In what ways could it be improved?

Knowledge or memory tests

One type of free-answer question provides a means of eliminating some of the dangers in taking too much for granted. By means of questions that reveal the respondents' knowledge, it is possible to sort out the "informed" group from the "uninformed." This unaided recall type of question may have other uses also. For example, to make sure that radio listeners have a certain program correctly identified, we might ask, *What do you particularly like about this program?* We would rule out those who say they like the comedy if there actually is no comedy in the show. The acceptable answers, however, would be useful to us not only as indicating correct identification, but also in establishing which characteristics of the program are most appreciated. The occurrence of erroneous impressions may point to the need for providing information on the subject.

Tests of knowledge on a free-answer basis range from outright tests to more subtle forms in which the respondent may not realize that he is doing anything other than stating an opinion. They may be designed either to classify people as informed or uninformed or to indicate the relative degrees of their information:

[40]

Who is the featured star on this program?

What day of the week is it on the air?

Can you tell me what is sold on the New York Stock Exchange?

What are the brand or trade names of some of the products this company makes?

Can you tell me where the plant is located? Where?

Do you happen to know what interest rate the bank pays you on this savings account? What rate?

Will you tell me what company you think makes Frigidaire refrigerators?

Do you happen to know what this is called? (Picture of roller bearing.)

Who puts out this magazine?

Can you name any advances made in manufacturing oil products during the past 15 years?

Can you give me an example of how a cooperative works?

How does a person become a member of Blue Cross?

As you recall it, what brought about this government regulation?

How many different services can you name that banks provide?

What are some of the ways the government makes use of banks?

Will you tell me what these new products are?

Would you tell me everything you remember seeing or reading in this issue?

What are the main ideas about the company that you get from this program?

What things did the advertising suggest?

Do you remember what any of these ads were about? What?

Who do you think pays for these ads?

Do you happen to remember what was said in the radio commercial?

Can you recall any facts that were given in the report, or any points that were brought out?

What do most dealers who handle the Brand-Line make call themselves?

What is the name of the water company here?

Source

Examples of questions that attempt to determine the source of the respondent's knowledge or of his opinions are relatively few. Possibly this is explained by the fact that they are seldom very productive of useful information. People cannot be relied upon to remember these sources. For example, few of us who think of Tiffany as meaning high quality or high price can tell where we first gained our impression. Nevertheless, here are some examples of wordings that have been tried:

Do you remember where you first learned about this?

Where do you get your information?

Where do you get most of your information about the oil industry?

Where did you hear or read that?

How did you happen to hear of it?

Information

Another kind of free-answer question asks for "factual" information rather than for opinions. In some cases the variety of responses to such factual questions may be as great as or greater than to opinion questions. For example, it was long ago found that to classify workers according to their reported occupations and industries is one of the most complicated tasks in any survey. Specialists, called occupational coders, have been developed to do this work and several volumes have been written on the subject. The *Classified Index of Occupations and Industries* used in the

Census is itself a manual of 300 pages. It employs five digits (as, V52-83) to designate each worker's activity.

On the assumption that only one answer is possible for each person, information questions such as these are not always thought of as free-answer questions. Of course, this would be true if people always stuck to simple facts, but in the case of occupations, for example, a worker may have several occupations—the actual work he does, the work he claims to do, the work his proud son claims for him, etc.

The real basis for calling these information queries free-answer questions, however, is simply that no particular choice of answer is stated to the respondent.

What is the principal purpose of your trip?

Where are you going on this trip?

What was the brand of disinfectant you bought last?

Which brands do you now have?

What are they?

What is the one main purpose for which you use it?

Would you mind telling me your name?

And your home address?

What kind of work do you do—what is your job title?

What kind of business is it—what do they make or do there?

What was your major activity last week?

Probes

Sometimes we are not satisfied to accept only the first answer given to a free-answer question. We may want to obtain all the ideas the respondent thinks of even though he doesn't state them all immediately. In such cases it is probably best to indicate to our interviewers the type of probing question to be asked, the chief requirement usually being that it should not influence the replies any more than the original free-answer question did.

Anything else?

What else?

Are there any others?

Give me any ideas you have.

On the other hand, we may wish to give more direction to the probing as in these three successive questions:

How could the street car company improve its service, in your opinion?

Are there any other ways they could make the service more convenient for you? What ways?

(If routes not yet mentioned): *Are there any changes in street car routings that you would like to have made?*

Precoding

With some free-answer questions, it is possible for us to establish in advance that the replies will fit into certain unmistakable patterns or to set up logical groupings for them. We may know that the analysis of data by age will be made according to three age groups—21 to 29, 30 to 44, 45 and over—and that further detail is unnecessary. Then, instead of writing down each individual's exact age, our interviewers can put an X in one of three age boxes printed with the question. In effect this shifts the task of coding such replies from the office to the interviewer (or to the respondent in self-administered questionnaires) and at the same time makes his job simpler because an X mark is easy to make.

It is extremely inefficient to leave for office coding any question that the interviewer can reasonably be expected to code on the spot. Every free-answer question should be considered in terms of whether it can be precoded, that is, answered by predesignated check boxes rather than by re-cording the answers verbatim. Justification for leaving any coding to be done in the office comes when the replies cannot be anticipated, when the desired grouping of the replies cannot be obtained otherwise, or when the coding is too complicated to be understood on a uniform basis by the

[44]

interviewers. It would be expecting too much of any staff of interviewers to code detailed occupations, for example, when to become an occupational coder itself requires intensive training.

The main argument for coding in the office, then, is to assure uniformity of treatment. It has often been asserted that interviewer bias is likely to enter into the process of field coding. A recent investigation (19) found that this is not necessarily true; in most cases field classification does not seem to alter the results of a survey. There is a tendency, however, for inexperienced interviewers to allow their biases to enter into the classification procedure more than experienced interviewers do.

On the other hand, the main argument for precoding is efficiency and speed. Another consideration that is sometimes overlooked is that the interviewer is better able at first hand than is someone in an office miles and hours removed to interpret correctly the intent of the respondent. It is not unusual to find that what appears to be an inconsistency in the recorded testimony of a questionnaire becomes a fully logical statement when explained by the interviewer. Explanation of such inconsistencies has on occasion changed the whole direction of a research project.

A compromise method of coding that has received little attention is one in which the interviewer both records the verbatim answer and makes the X box entry to be verified later in the office. This procedure may place the proper value on the interviewer's interpretation.

The precoded free-answer question is not a different kind of free-answer question in the sense used up to this point, but may actually be one of the several kinds already discussed. A few of the examples used earlier, in fact, could readily be precoded. Precoding does run particularly to answers that may be expressed in numbers, however.

How many persons in your family, yourself included, live here now?

How many of these persons are under 18 years of age?

What is the total acreage of the farm (or farms) you operate?

What do you think a bottle this size should sell for?

A nationally advertised brand of breakfast food sells for 15 cents. How much of that, would you say, goes for advertising?

How long does it take to get service and complete your meal?

About how many companies would you guess there are altogether in the oil industry in this country?

How long would you say a patent is good for?

About how much do you think you would spend for it?

How long have you been working at the place where you are now?

Do you know how much butter costs per pound?

About how many employees would you say the company has throughout the United States?

What is a reasonable per cent of profit for a company like this to make?

Another advantage of precoding in some instances is the possibility of indicating to interviewers the units of measure or particular terms in which the replies are desired:

About how much butter a week do you use just for cooking and baking?

( ) NONE   ( ) ½ POUND
( ) LESS THAN ¼ POUND   ( ) BETWEEN ½ AND 1 POUND
( ) ¼ POUND   ( ) 1 POUND
( ) BETWEEN ¼ AND   ( ) MORE THAN 1 POUND
     ½ POUND   ( ) DON'T KNOW

(Not cups, tablespoons, or other measures.)

What was the occasion?

( ) HIGH SCHOOL GRADUATION ( ) WEDDING

  ( ) COLLEGE GRADUATION   ( ) OTHER (Specify):

   ( ) BIRTHDAY   _____

    ( ) CHRISTMAS   ( ) NO SPECIAL OCCASION

    ( ) ANNIVERSARY   ( ) DON'T KNOW

Where have you usually eaten lunch during the past month?

    ( ) AT HOME, EXCEPT BOARDING HOUSE

    ( ) BOARDING HOUSE

    ( ) IN EATING PLACE OUTSIDE PLACE OF WORK

    ( ) ALL EATEN IN PLACE OF WORK

    ( ) PART EATEN IN PLACE OF WORK, PART OUTSIDE PLACE OF WORK

    ( ) OTHER (Specify): _____

Where have you usually gotten the food for the lunch you eat in the plant?

    ( ) BRING ALL FROM HOME

    ( ) BUY ALL INSIDE

    ( ) BRING PART FROM HOME, BUY PART INSIDE

    ( ) BRING PART FROM HOME, BUY PART OUTSIDE

    ( ) BUY PART OUTSIDE, PART INSIDE

    ( ) BUY ALL OUTSIDE

What is your biggest cash crop?

(Check boxes for this question should provide for the most common cash crops in the area and for an "other" or "miscellaneous" group of crops.)

Why are your present eating arrangements in the cafeteria unsatisfactory?

    ( ) TOO CROWDED

    ( ) SLOW SERVICE

    ( ) PRICES TOO HIGH

    ( ) POOR QUALITY OF FOOD

    ( ) OTHER REASON (Specify): _____

[47]

One last caution about precoding that also applies to any check box question is that the ideas indicated by the boxes should be mutually exclusive and reasonably exhaustive. Most of the above examples are satisfactory on this point, but the last one is certainly open to question. The interviewer is up against it if respondents say something like this: "Well, the price is too high for the kind of food you get." Should he check both price and quality? After all, that would appear to break this particular combination answer into two distinct parts, which is not the exact meaning of these respondents. They didn't say, "The price is too high *and* the food is no good." Nor do they necessarily mean that they would object to the price alone or to the quality if the price were right. In other words, it would be better either to take the answers verbatim or to include more check boxes in this case.

Wide open or not?

We have already noticed that free-answer questions may vary considerably in the amount of direction they give to respondents. They may be as general as *What do you think of the world today?*, or as restricted as *What did you think of the flavor of the watermelon you bought at Joe's Market yesterday?*

Sometimes free-answer questions are not directive enough. Floyd L. Ruch at the Central City Conference on Public Opinion Research discussed the question, *What kind of soap do you like best?* and pointed out that the word "soap" is not sufficiently directed (20). What kind of soap is meant— laundry soap, facial soap, or what?

Hans Zeisel has discussed how a wide-open free-answer question may yield unsatisfactory results because of the great amount of leeway it gives to the respondent (21). He goes on to say, however, that in making the question more specific we must not force the respondent to form and express an opinion on a topic to which he has not previously given any thought.

A wide-open question like *Why do you buy your milk at the grocery store?* will bring a variety of answers in a number of different dimensions. Some people will mention convenience, some will say that it is cheaper than having milk delivered, some will say that they always want to pay cash, some will speak of the small amount of milk they need, others will talk of how they can't predict their needs in advance, and still others will explain that they prefer fresh milk. But a more specific question like *What would you say about the convenience of buying milk at the grocery store?* may cause many people to state an opinion who never before have given convenience a thought. This is a case of giving importance to a thing just by bringing it up.

Two questions may be desirable in such a situation, one wide-open to bring out the relative importance of the spontaneous ideas, and the other more specific to indicate impressions of the single aspect.

Merits

Some advantages of the free-answer question were directly revealed as the various kinds were described. For example, the free-answer is uninfluenced, it elicits a wide variety of responses, it makes a good introduction to a subject, it provides background for interpreting answers to other questions. It can be used to solicit suggestions, to obtain elaborations, to elicit reasons, to evaluate arguments, to explore knowledge and memory, and to classify respondents.

Besides these fairly obvious advantages, the free-answer question has certain other attributes which we should not overlook. One of these is that it gives the respondent a chance to have his own say-so with ideas which more restrictive types of questions would not permit him to express. Courtesy may require that when we ask a person's opinion we should at least give him the opportunity to state the ideas on the subject that are uppermost in his thinking, even though they may not be important for the purpose of the survey. The respondent should be satisfied that our interviewer asks the right questions or else he may think we questioners are stupid—and in such cases he may be right. In this sense, the free-answer question has the best chance of being the "right" question from the respondent's viewpoint.

The free-answer question is of value especially as a preliminary aid in drafting other questions. For example, if we were preparing to make a study on international trade barriers, we could learn a great deal by asking a hundred people, *What do you think about free trade?* This question might produce 97 different answers and 3 blank stares. We could learn several things from these answers. Roughly how many people understand the term "free trade" as we mean it, how many have some other understanding such as the idea of haggling with a local merchant, and how many admit ignorance. The replies may also tell us the most common frames of reference that the term evokes—economic theories or political loyalties, specific industries or all industries, all foreign countries or particular ones, etc.

Thus, the free-answer approach is clearly indicated as a preliminary step to preparing questions on any unexplored issue. It points the way of least resistance or of most common understanding and indicates how familiar the public may be with the particular aspect we wish to explore. It can help to fill in some of the necessary conditions in later versions of the question, whether we come to a more restricted free-answer type or to an entirely different type.

In addition to all these functions, the free-answer question provides quotable quotes which may add sparkle and credibility to the final report. This richness is relied upon very heavily by some report writers.

Demerits

How can anything so good be bad? If the free-answer question has all these advantages, why do we ever use any other type? Well, the fact is that the difficulties with this type of question are almost as legion as its advantages.

In the first place, it is hard to enforce uniformity among interviewers in the way they ask such questions and record the answers. A very skilled interviewer may be able to obtain more information and to record it all verbatim while keeping the respondent's interest, whereas a less skilled interviewer may get little information, abbreviate or paraphrase it, and also allow the respondent's interest to lag. One may be able to take shorthand notes at conversation speed, while another just can't keep up with the talk. Paul Pry may hesitate expectantly after asking the question or wait for further remarks after one idea has been elicited. Curt Querier may rush through the interview, accepting merely prefatory "Oh, I don't know—" remarks as final answers. It is possible to augment one idea by five or six others through waiting for further elaboration or through skilled probing. One interviewer may take it upon himself to discard a reply that he considers to be irrelevant and then attempt to explain the question in his own words. Another may faithfully record an answer that is beside the point and never make the effort even to repeat the question for clarity.

It can be demonstrated that the amount of space allowed for the entry of the answer is enough to affect the recording of replies—little space, brief answers; ample space, lengthy statements.

In other words, although the claim is that these free-answer questions evoke unconditioned answers, it is possible, indeed almost certain, that the interviewers will influence both the quality and the quantity of the replies. In some respects the free-answer question, although free of influence in one sense, is the most easily influenced of all types of questions in this other sense.

Respondents, of course, range from the garrulous to the reticent and inarticulate. In a free-answer question, Gabby Prattler is likely to express himself fully, whereas Howie Falters may not state his feelings at all or only in cryptic fashion. Some respondents who say that they "don't know" may actually have reasonably well-formed ideas. This is true of other types of questions, but not to the same extent. The other types, through stating the alternatives, permit the less articulate respondents to express choices by giving them the necessary words.

Another problem with the free-answer question is that some respondents will neglect to state their most pertinent observations simply because they seem so obvious. For example, if we ask, *Why do you buy the 25-cent motor oil instead of the 35-cent oil?*, many respondents will neglect to explain that they are saving money thereby. We might find that only 40 per cent of the replies mention cheapness.

Some respondents, in a follow-up or reason-why question, will give answers which merely reenforce what they have already said. That is, they do not elaborate. They may say "I just think so," or "Because it is, that's all." Or when asked why they choose a particular basic industry as the most important, they may say, "Because it's essential." Or respondents may give irrelevant replies, or replies that at least appear to be irrelevant to other people.

All of these situations can present problems to the interviewer in an opinion survey. His attempts to place all respondents on the same footing may result in conditioning some of their replies. In practice, most research organizations prefer that the interviewer not try to improve on the questions. He is asked not to explain the question nor do anything more to help the respondent except perhaps to repeat the question in the exact wording given. In other words, emphasis is placed on stating the question as written and accepting the respondent's replies as given.

When it comes to the problem of what to do with the assortment of replies after they have been obtained, the attempt to make head or tail out of the multitude of answers to a free-answer question sometimes becomes a disheartening task. It is necessary to provide a means of making the answers comprehensible by classifying them in more-or-less definite groupings and showing the percentage for each grouping. Otherwise, even the person who has time to read through a set of a thousand or ten thousand answers is likely to become confused and to remember the unusual or startling replies more than the predominating, run-of-the-mill varieties. This coding, or quantifying, of free answers brings several other problems into sharp relief.

For example, few people will use the same words even in expressing the same idea. Some clarify their statements better than others. This makes gradation difficult when we want to distinguish between two closely related but nevertheless different ideas. Let us suppose that in a free-answer question about electric service two answer categories refer to promptness in appliance repairs and to promptness in repairing storm damages. What do we do with the incomplete but fairly common answer of "Prompt service"? We might squeeze it into one of the two established categories, or assign it to both at once, or consider that the individual may have been thinking about a different form of promptness such as no long wait in line to pay the electric bill. The safest thing, of course, is to set up another generalized "service" category to include such answers, but we may already have more groups than seems desirable.

A similar difficulty in coding is that sometimes a single word with more than one possible meaning appears among the answers. Suppose we ask, *Is there anything you particularly like about Crunchie-Wunchies?* Some people might give very forceful negative answers like, "Not a blamed thing!" Others might say, "Oh, I can't think of anything especially." Here are two different ideas, one a rejection of the product and the other just an inability to report any outstanding feature. We wish to make this distinction. All right, then what do we do with all the people recorded simply as saying, "Nothing." Some may have said this with great emphasis, but others probably did not. The one word has two important meanings here, but they cannot be separated.

Our coder is perplexed by irrelevant answers or those outside the intended framework of response. He has a problem also when one respondent gives five answers where only a single basic answer is wanted. Should he assume that the first idea given is the most important one to that respondent? The coder must have a thorough understanding of the subject matter. He must also understand various idioms and colloquialisms correctly because, while it is possible to make the question itself generally clear, the answers come back in all possible forms—slang, provincialisms, profanity, and worse. All the problems of written communication are compounded in the day's work of a coder. This is the reason that the coding of free answers looms as one of the most difficult tasks in the survey.

To sum up this chapter, we might say that the free-answer question is an "open" question in almost every respect. Its virtues and its faults all stem from this open feature. Its results are as full of variety as a country store, and just as hard to divide into departments.

4. Boy or girl?

A DISCUSSION OF THE TWO-WAY QUESTION AND ITS DUPLICITIES

AT THE other extreme from the free-answer question is the two-way question. Sometimes called the dichotomous or the bifurcated type, the two-way question is one which is intended to suggest only two possible alternatives. Yes or no, approve or disapprove, for or against, favor or oppose, true or false, good or bad, head or tail, black or white, this or that, left or right, male or female, higher or lower, Democrat or Republican—all these are examples of the choices that may be given to the respondent.

This type of question is by far the most commonly used of all. It appears to fit the largest number of situations. It reduces issues to their simplest terms and its advocates say that it comes closest to duplicating the types of decisions that people are most accustomed to making. And whether we realize it or not, it is probably correct that even our complicated decisions are broken down into many separate two-way issues.

The housewife goes into a well-stocked store to look for a frying pan. Her thinking probably does not proceed exactly this way, but it is helpful to think of the many possible two-way choices she might make: Cast iron or aluminum? Thick or thin? Metal or wooden handle? Covered or not? Deep or shallow? Large or small? This brand or that? Reasonable or too high in price? To buy or not? Cash or charge? Have it delivered or carry it? She has to make every one of these decisions, and what's more, when you question her, she can answer these as separate questions even though she may have lumped several decisions together.

The two-way question is simplicity itself when it comes

to recording the answers and tabulating them. Check boxes may be printed opposite the possible answers and numbered or precoded for mechanical tabulation. To record the answer a simple check mark or preferably an X is used. No coding is required and the card puncher merely punches the number printed next to this entry.

What are the important considerations in the use of the two-way question?

Implied alternatives

Both alternatives are not always stated in a two-way question. We may ask *Are you going to the game?*, without adding the alternative *Are you going to the game or not?* The assumption we make in the first version of this question is that the negative side is understood. Yet, even in such a simple case, the assumption may be challenged, as we shall soon see. It is also possible to ask a question without stating either alternative as in the one-word query, *Sex?* The many ribald remarks quoted as answers to this particular question show, however, that even it is capable of being misunderstood.

You will recall that in the three questions used earlier to illustrate the different connotations of the three words *might*, *could*, and *should*, no alternative was expressed. One of these questions was:

Do you think anything could be done to make it easier for people to pay doctor or hospital bills?

Now it happens than a fourth version was asked of another matching cross section of the public. It repeated the above wording, but the two words *or not?* were added at the end. The result was a drop of 3 per cent in the affirmative answers, from 77 per cent with the *could* wording to 74 per cent with the *could . . . or not* wording. With this size of sample, about 900 interviews in each case, the small difference is not necessarily significant statistically. Several repeated experiments would be required to demonstrate that stating one or both alternatives would usually affect the results. Fortunately, several experiments of this nature have been reported, some of them more conclusive than this example.

Cantril and Rugg show several examples (17), but about the most definite one is the following which Rugg describes in another paper (22). These two questions would appear to pose exactly the same issue:

Do you think the United States should allow public speeches against democracy?

Do you think the United States should forbid public speeches against democracy?

Certainly the opposite of "allow" is "forbid." We should expect directly opposite replies to these questions, but this is what happened:

First question		Second question	
Should allow	21%	Should not forbid	39%
Should not allow	62	Should forbid	46
No opinion	17	No opinion	15

Evidently there is something very forbidding about the word "forbid." People are more ready to say that something should not be allowed than to say that it should be forbidden. It would have been interesting to see the answers to a question stating both alternatives:

Do you think the United States should allow or forbid public speeches against democracy?

In any case, it is always safer to state both choices, in order to avoid the risk of the assumption implicit in giving only one. It is probably true that the risk may not be great with some questions, but with others like the one on avoiding layoffs, shown in the first chapter, the danger of misinterpretation may be very serious.

"Ain't fer or agin it"

To elaborate a little further on the need for expressing both alternatives, let us consider a question like, *Are you in favor of the nine o'clock curfew?* It would be a mistake to think that all those who say "No" are opposed to the curfew. It is true that some of them would be opposed, but others might not care one way or the other. Their "No" means only that they are not taking sides.

The question would be better stated as, *Do you favor or oppose the nine o'clock curfew?* This would give the split on active opinion and would allow the fence-sitters and willy-nillies the chance to say that they neither favor nor oppose the curfew.

Albert B. Blankenship has demonstrated (6) that those who reply "no" to the question, *Do you think that advertising is less truthful today than it was a year or two ago?*, do not necessarily think that advertising is "more truthful" today.

Or not?

The "or not" tagged on the end of a question to indicate the other alternative is not recommended for universal use. In some instances where it may be perfectly proper grammatically, the *or not* phrase may be confusing because it is an inadequate statement of the second alternative. Take the question: *Do you think it is all right for the government to make loans to business firms, or not?* Instead of thinking of the choice as "all right or not all right" some respondents may not see the alternative at all. They may misunderstand the question as stating only one alternative with the meaning "to make loans or not as the government chooses."

Wherever this type of confusion might occur, it is probably better to state the second alternative more fully than to use the "or not" phrase by itself. In the above case, the wording could be improved somewhat by simply making the alternative read: *or not all right.*

Two-way plus

While the two-way question suggests only two choices, it usually produces more than two kinds of responses. In addition to those people who make the desired choices, some people will say that they "don't know" or will not express an opinion. Sometimes such respondents will actually be in the majority. Even if we encourage them to make a choice by such devices as saying, *Of course, nobody knows about this. Just give me your idea.* or *Which way are you leaning?*, some will insist that they are undecided. A third check box should be provided for these answers.

Only two kinds of queries can actually be expected to result in just two answers. One kind involves certain factual items of the "it is or it isn't" variety or of the male-female type. The other comprises questions of knowledge or recall— a person either knows all the words of the "Star Spangled Banner" or he doesn't, he definitely recalls having seen the movie or he doesn't, etc. Even with questions such as these, it may be necessary to use a third category in the analysis— especially in the case of mail questionnaires where a respondent may neglect to make an entry. This third category might be labeled "Sex unknown" or "Not reported."

Hans Zeisel has described how it is sometimes possible to determine the correct answers for these blank items through interrelationships with other data (21). To take a very simple example from one of the above situations—if the mail questionnaire is signed, it is usually possible to establish the sex of the respondent from his "John Doe" or her "Mary Smith."

The "Don't know," "No opinion, " "Not reported," "Not ascertainable," "No answer," "No choice," "Don't recall" type of response necessarily converts most two-way questions into at least three divisions. But other categories also arise from some two-way questions.

Qualified answers

When we ask, *Are you going to the game, or not?*, some people will answer with qualifications or conditions: "Yes, if the weather clears up," or "Sure, unless my near-sighted cousin comes to visit."

Qualified answers like these present a very perplexing problem for which there can be no perfect solution. It can be argued that anyone who says "Yes, if . . . ," "Provided . . . ," or "Probably" is predisposed in the direction of going to the game and should be counted with the "Yes" answers. This argument is bolstered by the strong likelihood that some of those who do answer definitely in the affirmative may also have these same qualifications in the back of their minds. Although they may say "Yes," they no more intend to go to the game if it rains than do those who bring up this provision.

If this argument is accepted, however, the converse is also implied. Those who answer "No, unless . . ." or "Probably not" must then be classified as answering "No." Yet, very little difference exists between saying "Yes, if the weather clears up" and "No, unless the weather clears up," except perhaps a difference between an optimistic feeling and a pessimistic one.

Another method of handling the situation is to count in the definite categories only those who answer without qualification, while classifying all the others as "Don't know." Yet another possibility is to provide a "Qualified" answer box for those who insert provisos of any kind in their replies:

Are you going to the game, or not?

( ) GOING
( ) NOT GOING
( ) QUALIFIED
( ) DON'T KNOW

Anyone will realize that qualifications almost always arise, even in the most direct question. If we wish to force them into the nearest correct category, then we use only three boxes and let our interviewer decide whether an answer like "No, unless the weather clears up" should be counted as Yes, No, or Don't know.

If we need to have simon-pure categories, we may decide both to provide a qualified box and to operate on the question, thus:

Are you going to the game for sure, or not?

( ) YES, FOR SURE
( ) NO, NOT GOING
( ) QUALIFIED, NOT SURE
( ) DON'T KNOW

This last wording is intended to establish that only the definitely affirmative answers will be counted as unqualified Yes's. The qualified answers should include all those who admit a possibility of their going. The negative answers should include all those who have no intention of going to the game. The Don't Knows are those who either haven't thought about going to the game or who are not ready to indicate their leanings one way or the other.

Five for two

With some wordings there is no way of avoiding the extra categories arising from the two-way question. The questions may have two distinct types of qualifications plus the undecided category, as in this example:

Would you say that businessmen you know are optimistic or pessimistic about the business outlook for the next year?

( ) OPTIMISTIC
( ) PESSIMISTIC
( ) NEITHER
( ) SOME ARE OPTIMISTIC, SOME ARE PESSIMISTIC
( ) NO OPINION

Several things are wrong with this question, but as it stands five check boxes are required to cover adequately the types of answers it brings forth. The "Some are optimistic, some are pessimistic" box could perhaps be dropped if we asked about "most businessmen."

Qualified terms

The word "qualified" by itself is not always a satisfactory description of the intermediate position on a two-way issue. Like many other generalized terms, it will not often be used by respondents. About the only context in which it actually occurs is when the respondent says something like, "I'll have to qualify my answer." Therefore, preference should be given to descriptions which are more likely to be used by respondents in the particular situation. Some of these are:

IN BETWEEN	OTHER
NO DIFFERENCE	ABOUT THE SAME
BOTH	ABOUT RIGHT
NEITHER	SOME DO, SOME DON'T

Very often space is provided for the recording of the verbatim qualifications so that the various types of provisos can be studied separately or so that they may be shifted into the definite categories if desired. One way of indicating the need for such elaboration is:

( )OTHER: _____
(specify)

The middle-ground

Another problem with the so-called two-way question can be illustrated with the "about the same" type of answer. A question may be phrased to suggest only the two extreme positions on an issue when an intermediate position is also a definite possibility. We may ask:

Do you think that next year the price of shoes will be higher or lower than now?

Obviously here we must provide an "about the same" check box even though it is not mentioned in the question. Some, perhaps most, of our respondents will volunteer the idea that the price of shoes will be about the same next year. This two-way question is actually a three-way question by strong implication.

The problem is whether such issues should be left to read as two-way questions or should be expanded to three-way questions as: *Do you think that next year the price of shoes will be higher, lower, or about the same as now?* At first glance, the three-way statement may seem to be the better phrasing. Almost certainly, the answers to it will be different from the answers to the two-way version. Given the three-way question, fewer people will say "higher" or "lower" and more will say "about the same." This follows for two reasons. First, people have a tendency to choose the safety of the middle-ground reply and, second, the explicit statement of the alternative directs attention to it as a possible answer.

The middle-ground idea is often purposely left out of the question itself, however. The issue may be one on which people do not readily express opinions, and if the intermediate position were suggested most of them would take it as the easy way out. The direction of their leanings would be lost. In the answers to the following Gallup Poll question asked in June 1941, as many people volunteered the middle-ground idea as took sides on the issue (17). If the "about right" alternative had appeared in the question itself, it is likely that only a few extremists would have taken sides and the middle-ground replies would have bulked even larger:

So far as you, personally, are concerned, do you think the United States has gone too far in helping Britain, or not far enough?

[63]

Too far	15%
About right	46
Not far enough	32
No opinion	7

This suggests a criterion for use in deciding whether to state the middle idea. If the direction in which people are *leaning* on the issue is the type of information wanted, it is better not to suggest the middle-ground. Some literal-minded respondents, not knowing that any other answer is permitted, will choose one of the two stated alternatives even though they might prefer to give a middle-ground answer. If it is desired to sort out those with more definite *convictions* on the issue, then it is better to suggest the middle-ground. In either case, a box should be provided for the in-between answers.

Strength of alternatives

Statement of the two alternatives may vary from mild to harsh. This can have an effect upon the proportion of middle-ground and undecided replies. The less extreme the choices are the more will be the commitments, while the farther apart the alternatives are the fewer will be the commitments. Little evidence on this point has been reported, but question phrasers make constant use of the principle.

In the absence of documentation, I am basing the following gradation of a few alternatives on hypothesis. It is probable that the rankings might be incorrect by one or two places, but not that the relative positions would be completely upset when subjected to test. Any pair of these alternatives could be used in stating a given two-way issue, depending on how mild or harsh we wished to make the choice:

Good idea—Poor idea (mild, no commitment)
Prefer—or Not (mild, but more personalized)

Approve—Disapprove (mild, but suggests more consideration)

For—Against (harsh, but action not necessarily implied)

Favor—Oppose (harsh, suggests some action)

Vote for—Vote Against (harsh, requires action)

Demand—Reject (ouch!)

The alternatives do not have to be as simply stated as the
ones above in order to vary in harshness. The following
Gallup Poll experiment reported by Cantril and Rugg (17)
indicates that "changing the Constitution" is a stiffer alternative than "adding a law to the Constitution" is:

*Would you favor adding a law to the Constitution to
prevent any President of the United States from serving a
third term?*

*Would you favor changing the Constitution to prevent
any President of the United States from serving a third
term?*

	ADDING A LAW	CHANGING THE CONSTITUTION
YES	36%	26%
NO	50	65
NO OPINION	14	9

Again, the decision on which type of alternatives to
employ depends largely on whether we want to find all the
leaners, in which case a mild type is indicated, or only the
staunch supporters, in which case a harsh type will help to
push the leaners toward the middle-ground.

Complementary alternatives

Most two-way questions present directly opposing choices
and, therefore, the two sides are almost automatically complementary. We are not likely to set "good idea" and "oppose" against each other, for example. But as we get farther

away from the simple Yes-No, Black-White, and Favor-Oppose questions toward those that require a full phrase for a complete answer, we need to be on guard to make the two sides complement each other. Here is a question that does not meet this requirement:

Would you say it's better to regulate business pretty closely, or would you say the less regulation of business the better?

To anyone who is inclined to quibble—and quibblers make up a sizeable fraction of our population—this question presents a mild choice against an extreme one. "The less regulation the better" means, in essence, no regulation at all. It is small wonder that 31% of the school teachers who were asked this question gave qualified answers. We are dealing with a concept here that is not easy to grasp because no standard is presented for comparison. Whether business is already "pretty closely" regulated today depends upon your point of view—compared with Russia, "No"; compared with the 1890's in the United States, "Yes." It would perhaps have been better to ask:

Would you say that there should be more regulation of business than there is today, or that there should be less regulation of business?

The issue would be changed somewhat by this wording, but it would at least start everyone off from the same footing—the amount of regulation of business today. That is, it would if everyone understood how the words "regulation" and "business" are meant, which unfortunately may not be the case.

Uncomplementary exceptions

In spite of the obvious desirability of having the two sides of the question directly opposite, some exceptions have to be made. It would be foolhardy in a survey among school teachers to ask:

Do you think salaries of teachers like yourself are too low or too high?

The questioner would be more likely to retain the good will of these teachers by asking instead:

Do you think salaries of teachers like yourself are too low or about right?

Here, a typical middle-ground reply is converted into one of the two opposing choices, and with the very good reason that this approach is a very realistic one. It could even be argued that this wording is not an exception to the rule, but that in fact the question has now been made complementary.

One might ask why all three possibilities are not posed—too low, about right, and too high. The best answer is to refer to a question with three possibilities which has actually been asked of teachers. Even here the three choices did not include the "too high" idea.

In comparison with other lines of work requiring similar training, experience, and ability, do you think salaries of teachers are much too low, somewhat low, or about right?

Much too low	80%
Somewhat low	16
About right	2
No opinion	2

From these results, you can guess for yourself how few teachers, if given the opportunity, would be likely to say that their salaries are too high. The nearest thing to a rule that we can suggest here, then, is that the choices should be complementary at least to the extent of keeping within the realities of the issue.

Pie a la mode

It may seem unnecessary to point out that the question should set up choices that do not overlap, yet this principle of mutual exclusiveness is often violated. Some respondents could take both sides of a question like:

Would you say that the mayor is doing a good job of running the city or that he could do a better job?

It is entirely possible here that some respondents would say, "He certainly is and surely could." It is a little more likely perhaps that most people, feeling that both answers are right, would feel constrained to choose whichever one comes closest to expressing their general attitude toward the mayor. When you are asked, "What will you have for dessert—pie or ice cream?" it takes a bit of nonchalance to request pie a la mode.

Nevertheless, some people will say "both" when they are supposed to make a choice between two reasonable sounding alternatives, even when they are asked which choice is "more nearly correct." In the case of the following question, one person in ten answered that both were correct:

Which of the following two ideas about how to improve the American worker's standard of living do you think is more nearly correct?

> *The way to improve the worker's standard of living is for all workers to* PRODUCE MORE. *Or*

> *The way for workers to improve their standard of living is for them to* GET MORE OF THE MONEY *the company is already making.*

We should try for mutual exclusiveness in alternatives; but, failing that, we need to make provision for answers that combine the alternatives. It may even be advisable to include the "both" idea in the question itself, so that respondents realize that it is an acceptable reply. The decision about stating the "both" choice in the question itself is dependent upon much the same conditions discussed in relation to middle-ground alternatives. That is, it comes down to a matter of intent—whether we wish to force respondents to make a choice between the two alternatives or to allow them to take the compromise choice. But clearly in such cases we should give consideration to the fact that there are these two possibilities.

Sometimes an indefinite term may have much the same overlapping effect that overlapping alternatives have. Suppose that in interviews on Fifth Avenue we want to sort out residents of New York City and nearby suburbs from people who happen to be visiting the city. We could ask: *Do you live in or near New York City?* With most people this question would be satisfactory, but some residents of Jersey City just across the river might answer "No" and some people who live 50 miles away might answer "Yes." Other possibilities are: *Do you live in New York City or within 15 miles of the city?*, or to list the areas we wish to consider as suburbs. Still other solutions would be to ask, *How near to New York City do you live?*, or to go to the open question, *Where do you live?*

Twice times two

Even definitely stated two-way questions may give us trouble and lead to inconsistent replies if they are open to being misconstrued by respondents or if they result in answers which can be easily misinterpreted by our interviewers.

Is your health better or worse now than it was a year ago?

This question is grammatically clear enough but it does contain an unintended double choice: better-worse . . . now-then. The person who answers "worse" should, of course, mean "worse now than a year ago" but may actually mean "worse then than now." Clearly, this misspoken respondent is in the wrong, but this fact does not help the findings any unless his error is discovered.

This question can be improved so that it is less likely to lead to ambiguous answers.

Is your health better now or was it better a year ago?

In this version the unintended double choice has been eliminated. Instead of better-worse . . . now-then, this version has only the now-then comparison.

The unintended double choice can usually be avoided as in the above example.

What alternatives?

The greatest objections to the two-way question are that it limits respondents in their range of responses; it makes their replies seem definite when they may not be; it forces their answers to conform to the questioner's preconceived notion of the issue. In other words, the two-way question is at the opposite extreme from the free-answer question.

The two-way question is satisfactory so long as the two choices it presents are realistic. It is the type of question to use when the issue clearly divides people into two groups. The question about going to the game which we have used to illustrate some of the problems with two-way questions is an obvious case where this type of question is called for. One hardly considers the possibility of a free-answer question like, *What are your thoughts about going to the game?*

Merit versus seniority

A "good" two-way question will have only two possible sides if we disregard the middle-ground and no-opinion replies. If any other stand is possible, then either the issue is not clear or it just is not a two-way issue. Suppose we are talking about the worker's idea of whether merit or seniority has more to do with wage increases. We might start out on this issue with a question like:

In your company, would you say that most raises in pay are based on merit or that most raises are based on seniority?

This at first looks like a two-way question in that it states two sides of an issue. Yet, what if the workers think that *most* raises are based on favoritism, or on individual demands, or on flat increases given to everyone at once? Their answers, if given in the latter terms, could be squeezed into the qualified or no opinion boxes, but they might feel that they had to choose one of the two stated alternatives. You can visualize the misleading headline for this report "Majority of Workers Say Merit Governs Raises."

Still, aside from all other considerations, the relative importance seen in merit and in seniority may be a real issue. Let's try again:

In your company, which would you say is the more important in deciding whether a worker is given a raise in pay—merit or seniority?

This phrasing does state a two-way issue and it is less likely to result in a misleading headline. If we wanted to make it an even more definite two-way question, we could insert a phrase like *aside from other things*. Then, too, we might find it necessary to state "merit" and "seniority" in more down-to-earth terms.

Argument type

A very useful device for stating a two-way question on a complicated issue is to make an introductory statement which sets the stage for the question itself. Often this statement is given in the form of an argument like:

Some people say that, at the rate we are using our oil, it will all be used in about 15 years. Others say we will still have plenty of oil 100 years from now. Which of these ideas would you guess is most nearly right?

Another example of the argument type states only the one side of the argument:

A fellow talking on the radio the other day said that high

[71]

taxes on a company hurt the man who works for that company. Do you agree or disagree with him?

In these cases the arguments are put in the mouths of third parties so that the respondent does not feel that one answer or the other is the one that the questioner believes in. Thus the respondent is not influenced to give the answer that he feels will be most pleasing to the interviewer, but is forced to do his own thinking on the subject. This is important, because one of the failings of people, so far as opinion research is concerned, is the tendency to give what they think is a pleasing answer.

Generally speaking, the first example of the argument type is the better one to follow because it states both sides of the issue. Where only one side is presented, it is possible that respondents will approve that argument simply because they have been given no reason to disapprove of it.

Reversed alternatives

A "good" question, among other things, is one which does not itself affect the answer. Frequently, in an oral question which is difficult to understand, respondents show a tendency to choose the alternative they hear last. We shall talk at length about this form of bias in a later chapter, but one particular point is worth making here. It is that one test of a two-way question is to state the two alternatives in reverse order, *A or B* in half of the interviews, *B or A* in a matching half. The same proportions of answers should result on both halves. This demonstrates whether the order of statement has affected the replies, and furnishes a balanced result in any case.

It is interesting just as an experiment, but also worthwhile as a standard practice, to print two forms of the questionnaire for distribution to matching samples with the alternatives in the various questions reversed. For example:

FORM A

Do you think that next year the price of shoes will be higher or lower than now?

FORM B

Do you think that next year the price of shoes will be lower or higher than now?

If the order of stating the two alternatives has had an effect on the results, then the averaged percentages from the two forms will cancel out this effect. If we wish to take advantage of this cancelling feature in machine tabulation, we can precode the answer boxes so that the two sets of punched cards may be run at the same time, thus:

FORM A wording:		FORM B wording:	
1	( )HIGHER	3	( )LOWER
2	( )ABOUT THE SAME	2	( )ABOUT THE SAME
3	( )LOWER	1	( )HIGHER
4	( )NO OPINION	4	( )NO OPINION

In this way the answer boxes are placed in logical sequence to agree with the order of the respective questions, but all answers of "higher" will be punched "1" and all answers of "lower" will be punched "3" regardless of which form is used. Of course, it isn't even necessary to reverse the answer boxes on Form B, but it is usual to have the order of the boxes as nearly as possible in the same order as that in which the alternatives are stated in the question.

Reversing alternatives need not be carried to the extreme of awkwardness or where the switched wording might sound like a catch question. Little danger exists that we would ask: *Are you not going to the game, or are you going?*

Split ballots

I will have many occasions to recommend the split-ballot technique as a means of evaluating various question wordings. The idea of reversing alternatives which was just discussed is a good example of the split ballot. Most of the differences we have reported between one wording and another are based on this technique. Although question wording may be more art than science, the split-ballot approach is scientific experiment at its best.

This technique is a controlled experiment in every respect. When correctly done, we can say that the only variation we have allowed is in the wording we are investigating. Matching the cross sections of respondents establishes the degree of statistical tolerance in the results. Excessive differences between one form of the questionnaire and the other must then be due to differences in the questioning itself.

The split ballot is the one sure way to make progress in question wording—whether we are dealing with free-answer, two-way, or multiple-choice questions, or with distinctions among these different types.

5. Win, place, or show?

A DISCOURSE ON THE INTERMEDIATE NA-
TURE OF THE MULTIPLE-CHOICE QUESTION
AND ITS MISCONSTRUCTIONS

MULTIPLE-CHOICE questions are useful in two situations. The first of these is the case where the issue clearly splits into more than two parts, as blonde, brunette, or redhead. The second is the case where gradations are asked for, as in very tall, tall, average, short, or very short. It may sometimes be difficult to distinguish between these two situations, but the distinction is not too important. Where either variety or degree is under consideration, the multiple-choice, or "cafeteria," question has possible application.

Of course, if the variety can be restricted to two choices like merit and seniority in the preceding chapter, or if the number of degrees can be reduced to something like short and tall, then the two-way question becomes a possibility. At the other extreme, as the number of varieties or degrees approaches infinity, the free-answer question may be the best to use. It is the area between the two extremes where the multiple-choice question is indicated. For some issues it is hard to conceive of using any other type. There also are some special virtues in the degree type which will be brought out later in the chapter. For now, we shall concentrate our attention on the variety type.

Formality

If free-answer questions are the most casual type of query, then multiple-choice questions are the most formal. They are seldom used in ordinary conversation, probably because too much thought is required in posing them. We might ask a friend which candidate or which of the two leading candidates he favors for an office, for example, but we probably would not bother to enumerate the entire list of candidates in a single election. This very formality of mentioning every candidate, however, makes sure that none of them is overlooked.

This feature of the multiple-choice question—the listing of a large number of alternatives—does serve to call them all to each respondent's attention and thereby puts all respondents on the same footing. To illustrate the shortcomings of the other types: if we were interested in preferences for candidates, we might ask a couple of people, *Which candidate do you prefer—A or B?* The first person might say that he prefers candidate B whereupon the second might indicate that he prefers candidate X to either of the others. Then our first respondent might interject that he prefers candidate X too, but that he wasn't asked about him. Even in a free-answer question, this same situation might occur. Our first respondent might mention candidate B as his preference because of his idea that candidate X was not even in the running.

The dark horse

So in this illustration we have a variation of the old story of the dark horse. The most popular candidate could be passed over because his name is not on the ballot. At the outset it might seem just a formality to list the dark horse among the candidates, but in the end he sometimes wins the office. A properly constructed multiple-choice question brings even the dark horses into the light.

Our election example furnishes a good analogy of the functions of the three major types of questions. In electing a club president for tne coming year, nominations from the floor come in response to the free-answer question, *Are there any nominations?* All it takes at this stage is one mention and a second to each nomination; and relatively few members may participate in this preliminary discussion. Next comes the multiple-choice question when the nominees have all been listed and are voted upon by the entire club. Then, as the issue narrows down to the two leading candidates, a two-way question is used for the runoff.

The logic here is that like the nomination, original vote, and runoff vote, the three major types of questions perform useful functions representing different stages in the development of an issue. The free-answer question is useful in setting up the issue but may need to be asked of only a small number of respondents. The multiple-choice question is used on a full-scale cross section and brings all sides of the issue to each respondent's attention. The two-way type is also used in a full-scale survey if the issue narrows down to two major choices. The bootless argument of which type is better comes up only when the attempt is made to have one question do the work of all three types.

Different results

Not to run the analogy into the ground, but because it brings some lofty observations down to earth, let us hasten to point out that the nominations, the original vote, and the runoff obviously may show three different results. It has even happened in small organizations that in the voting a nominee does not receive even the two votes that were required for his nomination and second. The only case when all three results could be expected to be the same would be where only two nominations were made in the first place.

A number of experiments have been conducted, reported, and marveled at in which different results have been obtained on one issue from the three types of questions. All that needs to be said about those experiments here is that obviously the free-answer question on a given issue may elicit answers that differ from the answers to a multiple-choice question and that obviously the answers to a two-way question may differ from both of the others.

Card lists

To return to the subject of this chapter, when in a personal interview a multiple-choice question gets beyond three choices, it is usually necessary to hand the respondent a card on which the various alternatives are listed. It might be expecting too much to ask him to grasp so many alternatives orally. This is especially true when a number of alternatives are stated in sentence form.

One wag has remarked of the card that it is a means of excluding from personal interviews not only the deaf but also the blind and illiterate. This remark does point up a serious problem in the use of the multiple-choice question. The card list may require especially qualified respondents, and interviewers may avoid people who would have great difficulty in understanding the question.

To meet the difficulty faced by the illiterate or the weak-sighted, interviewers are frequently instructed to read the alternatives aloud to each respondent. Even if applied to those who are well able to read, this method helps by furnishing a double stimulus. Therefore it could well be followed with all respondents.

Cards are used once in a great while with two-way and free-answer questions, as in, *Which of these two colors do you prefer?*, or *What would you call the gadget pictured on this card?* By and large, however, the card is associated almost exclusively with the multiple-choice question. Sometimes the questionnaire will contain so many multiple-choice questions that to use a card for each one would create a problem for the interviewer, who has only two hands. In these cases a booklet may be used to which the interviewer refers the respondent by page number as he progresses from one question to the next.

Intelligence test?

One of the first reactions to the multiple-choice question is that it looks like a question on an intelligence test. For example, here is one asked during World War II:

Let me ask you which of these cities in Europe have been bombed by the Allies?

Card

This question was intended as a test of knowledge, and consequently does come close to being an intelligence question. One cannot help wondering how many people who did know that Schweinfurt had recently been bombed nevertheless gave an incorrect answer just as some people who really know better do give wrong answers to intelligence questions. No doubt some respondents become flustered in an interview and some are confused by so many names, all of which sound like reasonable possibilities.

It is almost certain that on nearly every question some fraction of respondents give answers which they do not really mean to give. This condition must be accentuated with multiple-choice questions. There is little or nothing we can do about the similarity of the survey questionnaire to the I.Q. test except to recognize this similarity. Some indication of the existence of the problem may be had through controlled experiments where a duplicate questionnaire is repeated with the same respondents.

In addition to this particular problem in human behavior, people exhibit a number of predispositions in their answers to multiple-choice questions. Unlike the I.Q. situation, however, adjustment can be made for most of these predispositions, or at least they can be made to cancel out.

1-2-3̌-4

One general inclination respondents show is that, given a list of numbers, they are prone to choose those near the middle of the list. This is especially true where any guesswork is involved in their answers.

To demonstrate this inclination to your own satisfaction, you might try a simple and amusing experiment on a few of your friends, one at a time. Ask each one to write down in a list the numbers 1, 2, 3, and 4. Then, while he keeps his list out of your sight, have him check one of these numbers. If past experience holds, you can then impress him with your mind-reading powers by stating that he has checked number 3. You will be right in the majority of cases.

2-4-6̌-8

It seems that if folks are going to guess, they reason that the extremes are not very likely to be the correct answers. Furthermore, they are usually right because we question worders do have the same predisposition—that is, we usually set up our list of numbers centering around the correct figure. Here is a knowledge test:

About how many trucks, of all kinds, would you guess there are in the United States?

Card	Answers
2 million	9%
4 million	24
6 million	36
8 million	20
No opinion	11

When the above question was asked, there actually were about 4,750,000 trucks registered in the country. So we see that the four alternatives were selected to center around this figure. Many of the 60% who selected the two middle figures must have been merely guessing at these "boxcar" figures, all of which may have been beyond their comprehension. With such data, the analyst has little chance of knowing how many of the reasonably correct answers represent outright guessing, middle-ground predisposition, informed guessing, and actual knowledge.

Now, here is a case where the correct answer is at one extreme. Starting with the fact that more than 90 per cent of all farm products leave the farm by truck, the choices were set up like this:

Of all farm products sold, about what per cent would you say leave the farm by truck?

Card	Answers
30%	5%
50%	12
70%	24
90%	55
No opinion	4

This time the analyst can be reasonably certain that a sizeable fraction of the people have a realistic impression of the importance of trucks in the marketing of farm produce. Enough respondents overcome their middle-ground proclivities and take the highest figure so that we can safely say they have a pretty good idea of the fact. On the average, about 14% select each of the first three figures. If as a rough approximation of the proportion who are merely guessing at the last figure we should deduct this amount from the 55%, we would still have 41% who were on the beam.

Therefore, it may be a wise precaution to set up any list

of figures for a test of knowledge with the correct figure at one of the extremes.

Incidentally, you probably observed that in each of these cases, only the four figures appear on the card. The "no opinion" category is not shown to respondents so that it will not be suggested as a possible way out, but it is given a check box on the questionnaire for those who do not make an estimate. This is the common treatment of such extra categories.

Two possible advantages of the multiple-choice question in the listing of numbers should be remarked here. In the first place, the card establishes the categories in the terms that are desired. Without the card the last question above would have produced a great array of odd percentages and miscellaneous answers of "about half," "most of them," etc. In the second place, the list encourages responses—only 4 per cent do not make a choice on the last question. It is always possible that in an open question some of the best informed may say that they don't know because they think they cannot give the precise answer. That is, not knowing whether the correct figure is 89% or 93%, they may say they can't answer. But when they see only four choices, the 90% comes close enough and they select it. If other people are encouraged to make poor guesses, the placing of the correct answer at the end of the list as in the last card furnishes an index of the amount of guessing.

Railroad stockholders

Not enough attention has been given to the influence that the particular numbers listed on the card may have on the answers themselves. The fact that these numbers do have some effect on the replies is undoubted, however, and the tendency to avoid the extremes is very evident. Let us look at one more example, just to show how little is known about the whole problem.

Railroad stocks are in the hands of approximately a million shareholders, yet some people think that railroad ownership is highly concentrated in the hands of a very few. For this reason, when testing knowledge of the distribution of railroad shares it is necessary to provide an extremely wide range of possible choices. Because of sheer length this list obviously cannot be an even gradation like 10, 20, 30, 40 and so on by tens to 1,500,000 stockholders. Here is the way this problem was approached in one case:

Which of these figures comes closest to your idea of how many people have shares of stock in the railroads in this country?

Card	Answers	
10	*	(less than ½%)
50	*	
100	*	
500	1%	
1,000	3	
10,000	9	
100,000	14	
500,000	21	
1,000,000	21	
5,000,000	13	
No opinion	18	

It is not difficult to reach the conclusion from these figures that a majority of the people realize that there are a large number of stockholders. But what influence does the list itself have on their judgments? Many people are shrewd in their reasoning. They certainly do not go through the mental gymnastics of the statistician—that this card list of numbers is highly skewed and that the numbers average out near 660,000. Nevertheless, about half of those who make estimates select the two numbers closest to this average. Perhaps they figure there must be some reason for having all the large numbers, so they discount the smaller numbers and make their selection from those toward the larger end of the list. It would have been revealing to use other numbers on other cards with matching samples of people, but this was not done.

Going to extremes

People have quite the reverse tendency from that displayed with a list of numbers when they are shown a card with a variety of ideas or statements. In this case, they seem disposed to select the statements at the extreme positions rather than those near the middle, and they favor the top of the list more than the bottom. Apparently they like to reach first for the first thing they see and then for the last thing that catches their eye.

In one experiment where several ideas were presented in different orders to matching samples of respondents, these results were obtained:

Idea A was selected by—

        27% when it appeared at the top of the list,

        17% when it appeared near the center, and

        23% when it was put at the bottom of the list.

Idea B was selected by—

        11% when at the top,

         7% when near the center, and

         7% when at the bottom.

Idea C was selected by—

        24% when at the top,

        20% when near the center, and

        21% when at the bottom.

Idea D was selected by—

        23% when at the top,

        16% when near the center, and

        18% when at the bottom.

In every one of these cases the idea was chosen more frequently when it headed the list than when it was at the bottom or near the center. On the average, the top position outdrew the bottom position by 4 per cent and the middle position by 6 per cent. The influence of the bottom position is not so definite, but on the average it outdrew the middle position by about 2 per cent.

The means of correcting for this type of predisposition is very simple. Just as was done in the above experiment, we can draw up a series of cards presenting the ideas in various orders. The first respondent is shown one card, the second another, the third yet another, and then this sequence may be repeated so that equal proportions of respondents see each card. Here is a question where three cards were used:

In which of these industries would you say there is the greatest competition among companies?

Card A	Card B	Card C
AUTOMOBILE	STEEL	OIL
OIL	AUTOMOBILE	STEEL
RAILROAD	COAL	CHEMICAL
STEEL	OIL	AUTOMOBILE
COAL	CHEMICAL	RAILROAD
CHEMICAL	RAILROAD	COAL

Of course, three cards are not enough to give exactly equal play to all of the six industries, but each does appear once at an extreme of the list, once at the middle, and once in between. Furthermore, the three lists are so arranged that the sequence is jumbled and no two industries appear together twice. The researcher may be reasonably sure that the possible effects of position have been fairly well cancelled out by this approach.

We do not have to print the questionnaire for these personal interviews in as many forms as there are cards. The list may appear in any one order on all the questionnaires so long as our interviewers insist that respondents state the idea itself rather than calling it "the first one," "the fourth one," etc. As a precaution to avoid this last possibility, the listed items usually are not numbered on the card.

You may wonder why this jumbling device was not suggested for the card lists of numbers. The distinction is that numbers have a logical order while these six industries do not. It is by no means certain that jumbling a set of numbers would correct for the predisposition to choose an average number anyway. And a disordered list of numbers certainly would be confusing to respondents.

Exhaustive listing

If other ideas than those shown on the card list are permitted to enter into the answers, it is best to revise the list to include the additional ideas. One of the strongest tendencies respondents display is that of making their answers conform to the choices before them. The fact that a small proportion do go out of their way to state another idea must be taken not as a full measure but rather as only a minimum indication of its importance. If we want to evaluate this additional idea relative to the others, we should add it to the list, where it will be chosen by many more people than the few who volunteered it before.

This can be illustrated with two questions having to do with royalty payments to unions for unemployment and health benefits. The two questions were not asked of the general public at the same time, but the results are so different that comparison for the purpose at hand seems justified.

The first question stated three choices:

Suppose they do set up a plan to provide workers with unemployment and health benefits through royalty payments. Who should manage the fund: the companies, the government, or the union?

A few people, totaling 15%, abandoned the three possibilities suggested in the question to volunteer one or another combination of the three. Here are the results:

Government	33%
Union	18
Company	18
Company and union	7 ⎫
Company and government	1 ⎬ 15%
Union and government	1 ⎪
All three	6 ⎭
No opinion	16

The 15 per cent nonconforming answers suggested that joint management of the royalty fund must appeal to many people, so that when it came to repeating the question later, the same preamble was given, but a card was used listing all seven possibilities. This time, far more people picked the combinations than took the first three choices.

Which of these should manage the fund?

Card	Answers
THE GOVERNMENT	18%
THE UNIONS	4
THE COMPANIES	13
COMPANIES AND UNIONS	18 ⎫
COMPANIES AND GOVERNMENT	8 ⎬ 52%
UNIONS AND GOVERNMENT	5 ⎪
GOVERNMENT, UNIONS, AND COMPANIES	21 ⎭
No opinion	13

It is possible that opinions may actually have changed from one survey to the next, but it seems more likely that the difference in results arises from the explicit mention of the combinations in the second survey as against the failure to mention them in the first. And certainly the combined form of management is a feasible suggestion.

The card list, therefore, should be exhaustive if we intend it to cover the range of possibilities. Otherwise an idea may be underplayed not because it ranks low in public thinking but simply because question worders either overlook it or happen to consider it insignificant.

Restricted choices

On the other hand, it may be quite justifiable to exclude an alternative from a list under certain conditions. In particular, an idea may well be dropped if it would obviously so dominate the answers that the importance of secondary ideas would be obscured by its presence.

The price factor is often a candidate for omission on this basis. If we are asking a question about the most important thing to consider in buying an automobile, a house, or any expensive commodity, cost is recognizedly a most important element. It may be unnecessary to demonstrate this. An open question on the subject might begin, *Aside from price, what would you say* . . . A multiple-choice question would start, *Which of these things would you say* . . . , and PRICE would not be listed on the card.

In later analysis of answers to such questions, it must be kept in mind, of course, that the original list was purposely incomplete. If this is forgotten, the analysis may rate the secondary factors as though they were the primary factors.

Multiple answers

The multiple-choice question is sometimes a multiple-choice in more ways than one. A respondent may not always confine himself to selecting just one of the ideas on the list, but may choose two or three. This is troublesome to the analyst who wishes to have things add to a simple 100%, because here he finds a total of 110 or 115 choices for every

100 respondents instead of one apiece. The problem is heightened in trend surveys if he finds 110 choices one year to compare with 100 in preceding years. To overcome this he may instruct the interviewers to check only the first choice mentioned, or he may use some random means of selecting just one choice for each respondent who has more than one box checked.

Some analysts show little concern over results that add to 110 or 115 per cent. Yet the occasional multiple answer in the midst of many single answers does indicate a certain lack of comparability in the thinking of respondents. It shows that they do not all have the same interpretation of the question. Probably some of those who restricted themselves to a single choice would have liked to name another choice also but, unlike the reservation jumpers, they held themselves down to one idea. What results then is a mixture of many principal choices and a few more-or-less secondary choices.

Our phrasing of the question can help in this situation by specifically calling everyone's attention to the fact that only one choice is required:

> *Which one of these . . . ?*
> *Which one idea comes closest . . . ?*
> *Which one is the principal reason . . . ?*
> *Which is the first . . . ?*

In addition, the card may be labeled "Choose One."

Or in those cases where more than one choice is definitely wanted or where it is intended that respondents should feel free to select more than one idea, our question might begin:

> *Which two or three . . . ?*
> *Which ones . . . ?*

Sometimes the interviewer is asked to indicate the respondent's first, second, and third choices by the use of numbers instead of the usual X marks, and the questions are so phrased. In any case, the whole point of this discussion on multiple answers is that *all* respondents should have the same idea of the mechanics of what is expected of them. To go back to the earlier analogy, a detailed election ballot instructs the voter to "Vote for One," "Vote for Two," etc. If this is a necessary instruction in conducting an election, it may profitably be adapted to research questions also.

Balance

The need for proper balance of the choices in a multiple-choice question is fully as important as in a two-way choice question. If the same idea is listed more than once or if several closely related ideas are pitted against a few unrelated ones, the list is unbalanced and the findings may be also. Let's look at an extreme case to make this situation clear:

Which one of these things would you say is most important to you in buying a new hat?

Card

STYLE
MATERIAL
GOOD LOOKS
APPEARANCE
WORKMANSHIP

Two of these choices—"good looks" and "appearance"—mean practically the same thing, while "style," despite what the fashion experts may say, fits into the same general category as far as many people are concerned. This question, therefore, overemphasizes one general characteristic of hats to the corresponding disadvantage of the other two.

Every item added to a list tends to subtract something from *each* of the other items in building itself up. It we had started the above list with only three items, "material," "workmanship," and "appearance," the addition of "good looks" would have reduced the mentions of each of the first three. It would have pulled down not only the proportion choosing "appearance," but also the proportions choosing "workmanship" and "material." The addition of "style" to the list would have pulled down each of the other four. The net result would be that in the five-alternative situation "quality" and "workmanship" would not receive their original share of answers while the other three ideas in combination would receive more than "appearance" had received originally. At the same time, "appearance" as a separate idea would itself have suffered a loss in comparison with the three-way question.

Cantril and Rugg have shown that the off-balance presentation of alternatives can appear to move people from one side of the fence to the other. In a study of isolationism, they used two interventionist statements and three isolationist statements in one list, but in another list overloaded the interventionist side with four statements as against one isolationist statement. Total choices of interventionist statements went up from 35% with the first list to 47% with the second while choices of isolationist statements went down from 24% to 7% (17).

All this shows the need for mutually exclusive categories and for balanced choices. Elimination of overlapping is one essential in achieving objectivity in the multiple-choice question.

Cases do occur, however, where the realities of the case are themselves out of balance in a sense. Such instances present very perplexing dilemmas to the researcher who wishes to remain objective.

Utility ownership

In the field of public utilities, such as gas, electricity, and water, many possible forms of ownership present themselves.

An electric company may be municipally owned, it may be federally owned as in the case of TVA, it may be state owned, or it may be owned as a consumers' cooperative. Against these various forms of public or semi-public ownership, the electric company may be, as most of them still are, a corporate business.

If the researcher has the problem of predicting the outcome of a municipal franchise election, it is easy enough for him to pair off city ownership against private ownership because that is the immediate issue. On the other hand, if he is faced with the general problem of determining how the public feels about all the various types of possible ownership, he then may have a five-way question:

> Business company
> Cooperative
> City
> State
> Federal

Here the usual type of structure, private operation, is ganged up on by four public or quasi-public choices. It is entirely likely that the overbalance of four-to-one will itself produce results wherein business ownership will receive only a minority of the total votes even though on a one-to-one basis it might have won out over each of the others by a substantial margin. Yet, the five possibilities are all real contenders. Each one is in operation somewhere in the country today.

This dilemma probably cannot be solved in a single question. A series of questions, each presenting two choices may be the only way to determine adequately how the public feels on this issue.

How many choices?

It is possible to show that few people are able to keep as

many as five or six things clearly in mind at one time. Hadley Cantril and Edrita Fried report a convincing demonstration of this in Cantril's book: They gave respondents a card showing six alternative statements, asked for a choice, and then immediately replaced the card with another on which two of the six statements had been changed and one had been dropped. Only half of the respondents could identify the changes and a mere handful located the omission (23).

From this and other experiments, a taboo seems to have developed among researchers against putting more than six items in any list. They reason that if a person cannot keep as many as six ideas in mind simultaneously, he should not be burdened with any more alternatives.

Such reasoning may be fallacious if carried into all applications, however. It would not matter much if we had twenty of Baseball's Greats in a list when asking fans to identify the Home Run King of all time. Respondents would look for Babe Ruth's name even if we listed a hundred possibilities. In establishing the most pleasing colors we could divide the whole range of the spectrum into six, twenty, or forty colors. In the larger group, the person who preferred blues could overlook the other colors and make his selection from among the five or six shades shown from that part of the spectrum.

These two examples should serve to clarify our thinking on the length of a card list. To be sure, people cannot keep twenty things in their consciousness all at once, but keeping everything in mind is not often a necessary requirement in making a judgment. There is then no special virtue in arbitrarily holding the number of items down to five or six.

Of course, there are practical limitations that should not be overlooked. A punch card in simple application allows a maximum of 13 categories in one column—1, 2, 3, ... 9, 0, V, X, and a blank. Allowing for simple combinations, two columns could be linked together to give 169 categories, and by a system of multiple punching it is theoretically possible to provide for 4,096 different combinations of punches in a single column. For simplicity, however, the usual application of the punching system may impose a limit of 12 or 13 items. This number of alternatives is sufficient for most problems.

Questions of degree

So far in this chapter we have been discussing primarily the variety type of multiple-choice question. From here on let us look at the degree or gradation type. In this type of question the alternatives might be worded this way:

Card 1

> a. It is absolutely essential to have a man like Truman for President.
> b. There may be some reasons against having Truman as President for another four years, but on the whole it is the best thing to do.
> c. While Truman has done some good things, the country would be better off under Dewey for the next four years.
> d. The reelection of Truman for another four years would be a very bad thing for the country.

Then to approach the issue from the other direction, the same respondents might be asked to choose from among these statements:

a. Dewey is just the man the country needs for President during the next few years.
b. Even though Dewey hasn't as much national experience as he needs, he still would make a better President than Truman.
c. Dewey is probably a capable young administrator, but he hasn't enough experience to be President in times like these.
d. The election of a man like Dewey at any time would be a very bad thing for the country.

Essentially, the degree-type question deals with two-way issues, but it usually spreads them out into two degrees for each side with or without a middle ground, thus making four or five alternatives. The question then becomes a matter of degree or intensity in addition to the matter of choice. The inclusion of mild and strong degrees on each side probably encourages some people who might not otherwise express a choice to select one of the mild alternatives, thus indicating the direction of their leanings. Those who select the strong alternatives would no doubt have answered a two-way question as well, but they now can safely be classified as being very definitely on one side or the other. The degree-type question, then, has the twin virtues of encouraging more choices and of providing a means of sorting out the staunchest supporters for each side.

Unless the main issue is clearly stated in all alternatives, however, the combination of the mild and strong on each side may not come out in the same relative position that a simple yes-no question would. In May 1941, when the public still favored staying out of the war against Germany and Italy by 66% as against 29% who wanted to declare war (No opinion, 5%), the Gallup Poll asked this question of a national sample (17):

Please tell me which of these policies you think the United States should follow at the present time?

Card	Answers
Go to war at once against Germany and Italy	6%
Supply Britain with all war materials we can and also use our Navy to convoy ships carrying these materials to Britain	36
Supply Britain with all war materials we can, but do *not* use our Navy to convoy these materials	46
Stop all further aid to Britain	7
Other replies	1
No opinion	4

Even if no other findings had been available, the Gallup Poll would not have taken the above results as reflecting war and anti-war sentiment in the ratio of 42% to 53%—the first two statements versus the last two. It is true that the second idea carried strong implications of war whereas the third leaned away from war. Yet people did not always see these implications, so that if it were intended to translate the findings into an assessment of war sentiment, at least these two statements would have to be reworded. The second might be, *Supply Britain with all war materials we can even if it means that we will go to war*, and the third might be, *Supply Britain with all war materials we can without getting ourselves into the war.*

This indicates one of the possible dangers in a degree-type question. Unless the alternatives all state the issue explicitly, the combined percentages cannot be expected to approach the same results as a two-way question. One other feature to be noted in the above example is that the two extreme statements received but small fractions of the total replies, 6% and 7%. In the degree-type question, then, respondents may tend to select the more moderate statements.

The fold-over

The degree-type question serves a dual purpose in the recently developed scale and intensity analysis technique, which technique will not be discussed in detail here (24). It is used first to classify people on one side of the fence or the other and second when "folded over" to reveal how strongly they feel about the stand they have taken. Frequently two separate questions are used to accomplish this result—the first obtaining the vote on the issue, and the second the intensity of feeling. A few examples of such intensity questions appear in the next chapter. But the degree-type question we have been talking about can be "folded-over" on itself to achieve the same result. Here is an example from a self-administered employee ballot:

If another company offered you a job at the same pay as you are now getting, would you take the job or not?

( ) I'M SURE I'D TAKE IT
( ) I'D PROBABLY TAKE IT
( ) I DON'T THINK I'D TAKE IT
( ) I DEFINITELY WOULD NOT TAKE IT
( ) I DON'T KNOW WHAT I'D DO

The first two alternatives are positive, the next two are negative, and the last is noncommittal. The first and fourth are of strong intensity, while the second and third are mild. This is a symmetrical question and is well adapted to the fold-over technique.

Another example from a style clinic showing a scale for self-administered questionnaires which is also easily adapted to the fold-over technique:

How would you rate this design for your own home?

VERY		POOR		FAIR		GOOD		VERY
POOR								GOOD

Any check to the left of a certain point is considered a strong poor, any check between that point and another point is a weak poor, and so on.

For personal interviews where arguments are presented for evaluation, a card may help the respondent:

The fellow on the radio says the highest pay should go to those who produce the most. Do you agree or disagree with him?—Strongly or not?

Card

AGREE STRONGLY	AGREE	NEUTRAL	DISAGREE	DISAGREE STRONGLY

A more intriguing adaptation of the technique involves a card which looks like this:

Card

| YES |
| yes |
| no |
| NO |

The respondent is asked to answer in terms of a "big yes," a "little yes," a "little no," or a "big no." If he should answer, "Well, yes and no," an intermediate box is provided on the questionnaire.

If at this stage the reader feels that the merits of the three major types of questions have likewise been stated in well-yes-and-no terms, then part of the objective of this book has been accomplished. An open mind is especially needed in research, and flat rules or arbitrary judgments might do more harm than good. One thing has always stumped researchers and will probably stump us for a long while to come: Having observed different results with different types of questions on the same subject, we still cannot agree on which of the different results comes nearest the "truth." As the development of phrasing now stands, it would therefore be a disservice to imply that any type of question is generally the "best" type.

6. How else?

DESCRIPTIONS OF SPECIAL TYPES
OF QUESTIONS AND THEIR SPECIAL FAULTS

IN ADDITION to the three major types of questions—free-answer, two-way, and multiple-choice—a variety of other types of questions and combinations of questions should also be taken into account. Most of these other types utilize the fundamental concepts of the three we have already discussed, but they differ either in application or in purpose, and therefore are appraised separately in this chapter. Some of these other types deserve careful consideration in their own right. A few are of dubious value but nevertheless need to be understood if we are to have a complete grasp of the subject.

Sleeper questions

In testing knowledge of a subject, we sometimes find it revealing to insert a fictitious name or nonexistent idea into the question or the card list as a control item. Surprising numbers of respondents will freely give apparently serious testimony about an imaginary idea, particularly if it sounds at all authentic to them. An experiment was mentioned earlier in which a gullible 70% of respondents gave judgments on a fictitious "Metallic Metals Act" (10). We have also referred to the 14% who thought that profits were based on year-end inventory. Such questions may be called sleeper questions.

Which of these brands of mattresses do you like best?

BEAUTYREST
SEALY
SLEEP HAPPY (Sh-h-h! No such brand. This is a sleeper.)
SLUMBERON
SPRING AIR
VANITY FAIR

When carefully constructed, the sleeper question gives some indication of the extent of guess work which enters into the answers on those ideas and things which do exist. By "carefully constructed," we mean that the sleeper should neither go to the extreme of sounding outlandish nor to the extreme of approximating an existent name or idea so closely that it becomes confused with that actual name or idea. On the one hand the name Beelzebub, Inc., would stand out as an obvious fake in a list of company names, while on the other Continental Pan Company might be taken as a misprint of Continental Can Company. In some embarrassing cases, a name chosen for a sleeper has later been found to be the legitimate name of some little-known company or product so that it was useless as an index of the degree of guessing. In yet another case, a sleeper was so well thought out that consumers chose it over existing brand names as the best name for the particular type of product.

Much the same idea has been used as a correction device in measuring the recognition of advertisements. Along with ads which actually have been run, we can include some which have not yet appeared. The proportion of people who say they have seen these unpublished ads gives us a means of assessing the amount of inflation in recognition of those ads which have been published.

Cheater questions

The cheater question is a device for detecting interviewers who fabricate, cheat, or "curbstone" their interviews. It is based on the theory that it takes a crook to catch a crook. I confess a temptation to cite concrete examples of the cheater question here, but even its strongest critics have so far scrupulously avoided giving the detailed idea away. Their reason is that some research organizations depend very heavily on this type of question, the value of which might be lost upon publication.

Intensity questions

Toward the end of the last chapter we discussed a degree-type question which through the fold-over technique served the dual purposes of classifying people on two sides of an issue and of ascertaining how intensely they held their respective opinions. More often, however, a separate single-purpose question is used to determine intensity of feeling. This type of intensity question usually comes after an expression of choice and may take several forms:

How much difference does it make to you who is elected President—a lot, quite a bit, or not very much?

How much difference has this shortage of equipment made to you?

Card

> It made no difference at all
> It's been a little inconvenient
> It's been a real inconvenience but no hardship
> It's been a real hardship

How definitely do you feel about this—very definitely, somewhat definitely, or not at all definitely?

How do you feel about your preference—do you feel sure about it or would you want more facts before deciding definitely?

Double-barreled questions

Generally speaking, it is hard enough to get answers to one idea at a time without complicating the problem by asking what amounts to two questions at once. If two ideas are to be explored, they deserve at least two questions. Since question marks are not rationed, there is little excuse for the needless confusion that results from a double-barreled question.

Do you prefer them short and dark, or tall and blonde?

Granted that this might sometimes be the actual choice a person is confronted with, nevertheless as an abstract question it probably produces more quibbles and qualifications than it does direct answers. The combinations of height and complexion given are only two of the many possible combinations. It would save time and discussion to ask about height and complexion separately, especially if there is no need to restrict the choice.

This is not to say, in situations where two factors are closely interrelated, that these two factors should not be linked together. For example, if we are asking about a 7-cubic-foot refrigerator vs. a 9-cubic-foot refrigerator of the same make, then price is an essential and closely related factor. We may still ask, without regard to price, which size is preferred, but before we are done we need to inquire about the 7-cubic-foot model at so much vs. the 9-cubic-foot model at so much.

An especially complex situation occurs when it is desired to test the acceptability of a proposed piece of legislation. The Dyre-Strates Bill may comprise 15 or 20 features, each of which has some importance in its own right. If we pose a single question lumping these features all together in one evaluation of the bill, we are in effect asking 15 or 20 questions in one. Almost anyone who knows the details of the bill would find it difficult to answer Yes or No without some qualification. Fortunately, in a sense, for the many such questions that have been asked, however, most people do not know the details of legislation so that they are quite willing to give their overall appraisal.

On the other hand, if a separate evaluation is obtained for each feature of the Dyre-Strates Bill and then an overall appraisal is requested, this appraisal is colored by the very fact that these respondents have now learned what the Bill contains. Because of their increased knowledge, they may no longer be representative of the public.

Claude Robinson solved this problem very neatly in his widely quoted, "The Strange Case of the Taft-Hartley Bill" (25). He began his interviews by asking some overall questions about this Bill which had just been passed. After the general appraisal, he asked about specific features of the Bill without identifying them as part of the Bill. The paradoxical finding of this study was that although the majority of working people said they were opposed to the Bill, substantial majorities also favored every one of ten major features it contained.

The moral of all this is that while justification can sometimes be found for an omnibus question, it is unwise to stop with it alone. It has to be followed up with separate questions about its several parts if full understanding of the opinion is to be obtained.

Symbolized numbers

Large numbers, sometimes called boxcar figures, are almost incomprehensible to many people. To these people 10 thousand, 10 million, or 10 billion all amount to infinite numbers. Yet it may sometimes be desirable to ask their judgments in terms of choices among such boxcar figures. One possible way of approaching this problem is suggested in a question asked in a survey for one large company.

It was recognized that the public would think of this company as a large company, but the question was, how large? Sales and capitalization both are tremendous figures to visualize, and even the number of employees is too large to be readily comprehended. The question which was finally used was basically in terms of number of employees, but each number was symbolized by associating it with a well-known company name. The question read something like this:

Which of these companies would you say it comes closest

to in the number of employees it has—General Motors with 350,000 employees, Sears, Roebuck with 70,000, National Cash Register with 12,000, or Florsheim Shoe with 3,000?

It is not possible to say whether most respondents answered in terms of the numbers or in terms of their general impressions of the four companies named. This type of question has not been used very often, but it is mentioned here in the hope that others will experiment further with symbolized numbers.

Or what?

The catch-all phrase "or what" may be tacked onto the end of a two-way or multiple-choice question, thus converting it to a mixed form of free-answer question. You will recall the question on profits which I quoted in Chapter 2:

When you speak of profits, are you thinking of profit on the amount of sales, on the amount of money invested in the business, on year-end inventory, or what?

In some cases the "or what" ending is a useful device, but in others it may lead to erroneous conclusions. The two technically correct answers to the above question are that profit is figured on sales or on investment. Knowledge of these two bases for computing profits is all that is being tested. The "or what" is added to give opportunity for expression of other concepts that may be in some people's thinking. It prevents forcing their answers into the first three pigeonholes and probably is justified in this case.

Or, we may be interviewing 18-year-old boys who are enrolled in schools. We would expect most of them to be attending either high school or college, but a few might conceivably still be in grade school or junior high school and some would be attending a trade school like a barber college. Our question might read:

Are you attending high school, a university, or what?

The boxes for this question could be:

( ) HIGH SCHOOL
( ) UNIVERSITY
( ) OTHER (specify) :————————

Again, the "or what" is probably justified in the above type of factual question where a wide miscellany of answers will be given by a small minority of respondents.

Sometimes, however, in an opinion question the "or what" phrase is a faulty compromise between the two-way or multiple-choice question and the free-answer question. It might read like this:

In your company what would you say decides whether a person is to get a raise in pay—merit, seniority, or what?

The somewhat fallacious reasoning behind this question is that if the respondent sees any other considerations besides the two that are stated, he has the chance to express them in the "or what" category. It is intended that any ideas other than merit or seniority will be reported verbatim. But, like many compromises, this combination is neither fish nor fowl.

It does not give the same result as a free-answer question because it directs attention to two specific alternatives and loads them up with more answers than if they had not been suggested. Conversely, it does not produce so high a proportion of other specific ideas as would either a free-answer question which states no alternatives or a multiple-choice question which states these other alternatives. Answers to the question, therefore, could lead to incorrect interpretation if accepted as being the same as free answers. Thus, we see that the "or what" phrase can lead to erroneous conclusions if it is taken too seriously as having brought out all the answers.

Successive eliminators

One type of question which can influence judgments of respondents and analysts alike is the follow-up type which breaks down one side of the opinion while accepting the other side. I hasten to illustrate with an obviously absurd example.

Do you prefer pumpkin pie or mince pie?

Mince pie	60%
Pumpkin pie	30
No opinion	10

Do you mean that you prefer mince pie cold or hot, or that you prefer it only when it is hot. Asked only of the 60% who say they prefer mince pie.

Either cold or hot	40%
Only when hot	10
Undecided	10

Do you really prefer mince pie hot or cold or would you just as soon have pumpkin pie? Asked only of the 40% who say they prefer mince pie hot or cold.

Really prefer mince	15%
Just as soon have pumpkin	15
No opinion	10

Erroneous Conclusion: While most people (60%) "say" that they prefer mince pie over pumpkin pie, only a small proportion (15%) actually do prefer mince pie.

By means of successive eliminators it is possible to tear down an original opinion until only its most firm defenders remain. If such is the researcher's intention, it is right to use this type of question, but if he falls into the trap of assuming that the original opinions are thereby proved wrong, he is wrong. If you have occasion to use successive eliminators, it is wise to use them to tear down not one side alone, but both sides of the original question. In the above example, comparable questions should be asked of those who originally choose pumpkin pie to see how strongly they adhere to their preference.

Serialized questions

Where a series of questions all having the same introduction and the same alternatives is used, it may be unnecessary and even irritating to repeat the introduction and alternatives with each one. It is entirely satisfactory to set up a series of questions like this group from a survey on military recruitment:

Let's suppose for a minute that you actually were going to enlist. I'll ask you about several branches of military service and you tell me how you would feel about being in each one, according to the four ideas shown on this card—

Card

> WOULD LIKE IT
> ALL RIGHT
> WOULDN'T LIKE IT
> DON'T KNOW MUCH ABOUT IT

If you were enlisting, how would you like to be in the Infantry?
How about the Field Artillery?
How about the ground crew in the Air Force?
How about the flight crew in the Air Force?
How about the Signal Corps?
etc.

Questions in series like this one usually move very fast. The substitution of "How about" in place of the original phrasing is all right provided the original question is understood to apply throughout. In fact, the "How about" can be eliminated for the later questions, in which case they come down to the simplest form:

The ground crew in the Air Force?
The flight crew in the Air Force?
The Signal Corps?
Ordnance?

Mechanized Cavalry?
etc.

If the list is very long, however, it may be well at different places in the series to repeat the entire question to insure that the issue is still understood. Every fourth or fifth question might be amplified to:

If you were enlisting, how would you like to be in the Signal Corps?

In Ordnance?

Mechanized Cavalry?

Combat Engineers?

If you were enlisting, how would you like to be in the Military Police?

The Medical Department?

etc.

Which-is-the-whatest

A very useful device for obtaining comparative evaluations of companies or industries has been dubbed the "which-is-the-whatest" approach. To take a simple case, residents of a manufacturing community are handed a card which lists the largest plants in the community and then are asked a series of questions like:

Which one of these companies do you know most about?

Which one would you recommend to a friend who was looking for work?

From the answers to a comprehensive series of such questions, it is possible to depict the popular profiles or stereotypes for each of the companies. Company A's strong point is its reputedly high wages, but Company D is more likely to be recommended as a place to work because it is thought to provide steadier employment, etc.

Until recently, however, this approach has had one serious drawback. The difficulty arose from the fact that people have a strong tendency to name the company they know best as the "whatest" on every positive attribute. The companies that are not well known are usually rated far down the list on such questions. Only in instances where the small company has some really outstanding characteristic is it likely to receive as many or more mentions than the large company.

An article in *The Public Opinion Quarterly* presents a theory originally based on a study of six communities and a total of 48 companies (26). The hypothesis stated there is simply that all other things being equal, the proportion of mentions of a company are directly related to its size as expressed by its share of the total employees of all companies on the list.

Here in the first column we see the proportion of residents in one community naming each of four companies as the best place to work. For comparison, the second column shows the percentage distribution of employees among those companies. Company A is almost four times the size of Company B and fifteen times as large as Company C. Company D has only 1% of the total payroll of the four companies:

	Residents saying it is the best place to work	Distribution of employees
Company A	79%	74%
Company B	16	20
Company C	4	5
Company D	1	1
Total	100%	100%

If we were to consider only the first column of answers here, our conclusion might be that Company A has done an excellent job of convincing the community of its merits as an employer. But comparison with the second column indicates that its evaluation by the community is only 5 percentage points above what would normally be expected for a company of its relative size.

Now let us look at six companies in another community as rated on this same question:

	Residents saying it is the best place to work	Distribution of employees
Company E	70%	75%
Company F	12	10
Company G	9	5
Company H	5	5
Company I	2	3
Company J	2	2
Total	100%	100%

In this second community we see that, while Company E is by far the most often mentioned as the best place to work, it does not receive the high proportion of mentions that its par for size shows to be normal. On the other hand, Company G which is a much smaller company is mentioned more frequently than would be expected if all other things were equal. Our evaluation of the community's appraisal of companies, therefore, is altered when we adjust for the predisposition toward naming the largest company.

It is unlikely that a means will ever be found of changing the wording of the which-is-the-whatest question to eliminate the tendency to name the best-known company. The comparison by size, however, whether in terms of number of employees, amount of investment, sales in dollars or in items, or by other appropriate measures, gives us a means of correcting for this tendency. If nothing else, the above examples should serve to put us on guard against jumping at conclusions from the unadjusted answers to questions of this type.

Quintamensional design

We have proceeded far enough now to be able to glance at the way various types of questions may be interwoven to produce a rounded appraisal of a respondent's thinking on a given subject. George Gallup has dubbed one particular combination of questions the "quintamensional plan of question design" because it approaches any topic from five different paths (16). He does not argue that five questions are always needed or that five questions are always sufficient, but does show how five questions can be used to cover the most essential features of an opinion.

Awareness of the topic is first ascertained by a free-answer knowledge question. *Uninfluenced attitudes* on the subject are next developed in a free-answer question. *Specific attitudes* are then elicited through a two-way or a multiple-choice question. *Reasoning* behind the attitudes follows in a free-answer reason-why question. *Intensity* of feeling comes last in an intensity question such as those discussed earlier.

Application of the quintamensional design to a particular topic is well illustrated by Dr. Gallup in a series of questions about the time-honored practice of filibustering:

1. *Will you tell me what a "filibuster in Congress" means to you?* (Free-answer knowledge)

2. *What, if anything, should Congress do about filibusters?* (Free-answer attitude)

3. *It has been suggested that the Senate change its rules so that a simple majority can call for an end to discussion instead of a two-thirds majority as is now the case. Do you approve or disapprove of this change?* (Two-way choice)

4. *Why do you feel this way?* (Reason-why)

5. *How strongly do you feel about this—very strongly, fairly strongly, or not at all strongly?* (Intensity)

The chief contribution of the quintamensional design is its formulation of five essential factors in an opinion. It should not be followed blindly because frequently one question is sufficient for the purpose at hand and sometimes the issue is too complex for a half-dozen questionnaires. Nevertheless, it is always advisable to keep in mind these five elements—awareness or familiarity with the issue, expression of individual attitudes, reactions to the specific proposal, reasons for these opinions, and intensity of the opinions.

7. Still beat your wife?

A SERMON ON THE CARE AND TREATMENT OF RESPONDENTS

PEOPLE are being exceedingly gracious when they consent to be interviewed. We may ask them to give us anywhere from a few minutes to many hours of their time in a single interview. We may ask them to expose their ignorance with no promise of enlightenment. We may try to probe their innermost thinking on untold subjects. We may sometimes request their cooperation before telling them who the sponsor is and before indicating the nature of our questions—for fear of prejudicing their answers. All this, yet they submit to being interviewed. And without promise of even a penny for their thoughts!

The respondent may feel flattered that we are asking his opinions, and his vanity probably adds to his willingness to be questioned. He may take some pride in being singled out for the dubious honor of having his opinions recorded. Despite the many surveys and the fact that his ideas are not separately important, he nevertheless is somewhat justified in his feeling of uniqueness, because only a fraction of the total population ever participates in surveys. He is also curious to find what these polls are all about and to see what kinds of questions are going to be asked. Or he may just want to talk and to impress people. Whatever his motives, we should keep in mind that he is the one who is doing us the favor. He condescends to receive us.

Free speech

Free speech works both ways. To be sure, we have the right to ask the questions. The respondent, on the other hand, has every right to refuse to answer them. And sometimes it seems that we do everything we can think of to induce refusals. We approach complete strangers, ask them a battery of impertinent questions, blindfold them, stick strange concoctions under their noses, and refuse to elaborate on the meaning of the questions on the assumption that explaining them might affect the answers. The surprising thing about it all is the small number of turn-downs we receive.

Perhaps this signifies that if we want to we can ask a question in any way we choose and get away with it. But if we keep in mind the ordinary rules of courtesy and good manners, we can easily avoid giving offense. The interview might as well be a pleasant experience all around. There is seldom any real need to trip up the respondent, to ask him confusing questions, to talk down to him, or to sell him an idea. And if we don't do these things purposely, we should be careful not to slip into them unconsciously.

Talking down

Survey questions ideally should be geared to embrace all levels of understanding so that they have the same meaning for everyone. The obvious means of achieving this ideal is to adapt the wording to the understanding of the lowest educational levels. Surprisingly enough, this can usually be done without giving the patronizing appearance of talking down to them and without sacrificing clarity at other levels.

However, most of us who are in the business of wording questions happen to be college-trained and we sometimes find it difficult to express ourselves in fourth-grade terms. We either neglect the person with grammar-school education and talk far over his head, or we apparently become over-zealous to translate for this primitive creature and so indulge in intellectual baby talk.

This talking down may take several forms, one of which consists of the explicit definition of terms in common use.

Granted that this explanation may be needed for some people, it still does not have to be an undisguised definition. Just to help the one person in ten who does not readily understand the term "income tax," it would be an insult to the other nine to ask them all this open question:

How do you feel about your income tax—that is, the amount you have to pay the government on the money you take in during the year?

This very evident attempt at explanation tells all interviewees that we assume they do not understand the term. How much better it would be to ask it like this!

How do you feel about the amount you have to pay the government on the money you take in during the year—your income tax, that is?

Now we have something that doesn't sound at all like an explanation. It appears more like normal conversation—as though the questioner, while groping for the particular term to use, ad libbed an alternate description, then finally remembered the term in time to sum up his question. It will not be so likely to offend any of our ten respondents.

For quick practice, you might try the simple inversion of term and explanation to explanation and term with ideas like consumer cooperatives, jurisdictional dispute, chamber of commerce, unemployment compensation, or grievance.

As a milder illustration of talking over people's heads, talking down to them, and of the middle course, we can take this knowledge question:

Have you ever heard of the Tennessee Valley Authority?

This wording is pitched a little too high. Some respondents may be chary of answering "Yes" because they are not sure whether the agency is actually called an "Authority" or an "Administration." Others who have heard the more commonly used expression, "TVA," may not know that it is synonymous with Tennessee Valley Authority. In other words, the affirmative answers to the question may give an understatement of the people who are aware of TVA and its activities.

Now, let's try to make it more understandable:

Have you ever heard of the TVA, that is, the Tennessee Valley Authority?

No doubt this is more generally comprehensible, but it is pitched too low. It talks down to people. It explains the initials, which is entirely unnecessary for those who know what the initials mean. To them it is noticeably redundant and may give some slight offense. If we are correct in our assumption that "TVA" is better known than "Tennessee Valley Authority," then we are using the less well known to explain the better known. The result is anti-climax as well as talking down. Now, let us try this one in reverse:

Have you ever heard of the Tennessee Valley Authority, that is, the T.V.A?

No one should be offended by this, and all formalities are observed. We give the proper name, and then, as though an afterthought, the more popular nickname. We still get in both our shots and can use either reference in subsequent questions.

Now, to answer some questions which you may have been wanting to ask about this TVA example. First, "Isn't it talking down to ask people if they have heard of something as highly publicized as the TVA has been?" Maybe so, but in national cross sections of the public more than a fourth have usually said "No" even to the third version of our question! Second, "If TVA is a more popular name than Tennessee Valley Authority, why bother to use anything but the three initials?" This suggestion might be a good one if it were not for the fact that some people confuse TVA with TWA, even in the third version of our question!

From the experience with the wording of the questions about the income tax and TVA, we can deduce a principle. If an elaboration or explanation of a common term is needed in a question, it is generally better not to mention the term until after the explanation has been given.

Or ain't it?

Some beginners at question wording strain so hard in making their questions comprehensible to hoi polloi that they become positively and purposefully ungrammatical. Apparently they reason that the way to speak to the masses is to use the "dem an' dose" language of the comic strips. Needless to say, this is the worst kind of talking down. Such wording does not appeal to large parts of the public, and therefore lacks the universality that good questions should have.

Would it be good if there was a rule to give everyone in the outfit you work for their lunch without them having to pay for it?

This wording, especially if the interviewer could say it in character, might go unnoticed by many people. But, if coming from a school-teacherish interviewer, it might sound out of place even to some people who ordinarily massacre grammar this way themselves. Furthermore, there is no need to make the idea of free lunches so complicated. You can easily state the issue forthrightly in half as many words.

Ending with a proposition

On the other hand, we usually do want to maintain a conversational tone in our interviews, and it is probably true that people tend to be somewhat less grammatical in their oral questions than in written statements. Precise grammar in a question may sometimes appear stilted. *"Whom do you love?"* may set up a slight obstacle in the way of eliciting the desired answer! There may be good reason for neglecting the possessive case before a gerund, for using superlatives in a two-way question, or for leaving out connectives. In cases like the following, the questions may sound more natural to almost everyone than they would if the rules of grammar were strictly observed as indicated by the parenthetical items.

Have you heard any talk about the city('s) taking over the trash collection service?

Which are the most (more) courteous—the salesmen or the repairmen?

Do you think (that) popcorn is better (than) or not as (so) good as peanuts?

Utsnay

Another dubious way of establishing rapport at the respondent's level is to use slang expressions. The trouble with slang is that it is ever-changing and not universally understood. For the initiated, it may be more expressive than other speech, but sometimes relatively few people are in the know. Even when used in questions to be asked among particular groups, the degree of understanding may be highly variable. Not every bobby-soxer is a hepcat. Not every student talks pig-Latin. Probably few sailors understand all the terms in the Navy section of *The American Thesaurus of Slang* (27). The thing to blow wise to about slang is that it ain't Jerry to all hands and the cook.

Folksiness

In the effort to use a conversational tone, one is sometimes tempted to use homey-sounding colloquialisms, provincialisms, or metaphors. Like slang, the colloquialism sometimes seems more expressive than straight talk does. It is doubtful, however, whether provincial or colloquial speech has any great advantage even in talking with habitual users. In some parts of the country where "the electric" is commonly used for "electricity," the latter term is understood as well. Elsewhere, reference to "the electric" would sound very quaint. Thus it seems just as well to employ the correct terminology everywhere.

Another problem with some common idioms and metaphors is that they have not only their idiomatic meanings but also some puzzling literal interpretations. Here are a few examples pointed up slightly to emphasize the fact that some common expressions can have strange literal or mixed meanings:

Would you feel put out if you were evicted?
Do you have the right slant or are you a left-winger?
Did you get the connection or miss the party?
Do you ever get down on the farm?
Can you put up with vinegar?
When did you last see a doctor?

You don't have to do very much interviewing to find that some people just do not understand the folksy kind of talk and so give their answers within the strict terms of the King's English. They miss the boat but you are the one who gets stranded.

Censored

You may not have much use for people who are always finding something off color in innocent statements, or for those who see a double meaning in every single question, or for chronic punsters generally. Yet such people can perform a very useful function in question wording. Just as the movie industry established a board of censors to police its films against improprieties, so do we need to alert ourselves against possible *double entendres* in our questions.

We can save embarrassing the respondent and the interviewer if we recognize the various possibilities in a phrase and then make the necessary changes to overcome our innocent errors of commission. If you happen to be an able punster, you will detect possible misunderstandings which the strictly literal person might overlook.

I just mentioned *The American Thesaurus of Slang.* You may understand better what I mean when you refer to the index of that volume, where a simple word like "put," alone and in combination with other words, is given ten columns of paragraph references. No one would put up with all those ideas in his mind at once, but if you could put your finger on at least the more obvious double meanings you would have some advantage in putting out clean-cut questions.

How specific?

One of the enigmas of asking questions comes in the problem of qualification, amplification, or description. Once we have stated the question in simple terms for the grade-school mind, what if it is incomplete for those with higher educations? For example, we have pointed out earlier that many people are willing to make judgments on profits without going into the refinements of accounting terms. But some others do not like to commit themselves without knowing specifically what profits they are talking about.

Many workers will not object to a question like this:

What per cent of profit would you say that your company made last year?

But some may ask, "Profit on what basis?" For these we might want to state the question thus:

What per cent of net profit on sales would you say your company made last year?

or even—

What per cent of net profit on sales before taxes would you say your company made last year?

The latter two wordings may be better ones for general use, on the theory that the clarifying words probably do not greatly disturb the people who do not require the distinction. Insertion of the words "retail" and "complete" in these next questions may be a matter of indifference to most people but of some help to the quibblers, who make up a sizeable proportion of the public.

What is your idea of how retail gasoline and oil prices are decided?

Are you in favor of complete prohibition?

On the other hand, the unneeded insertion of explicit words can greatly alter the connotation of a question.

How do you like swimming in the ocean?
is quite different in implication from—

How do you like swimming in the Atlantic Ocean?
Ask any Californian!

Unintended specificity can also cause trouble, as in a case reported in a Czechoslovakian poll which asked what was intended as an inventory question:

How many books do you have on your bookshelf?
Comparison with book sales and other indications showed that this question was giving an undercount of books in homes because many people in Czechoslovakia as well as here keep their books elsewhere than on bookshelves.

Over-elaboration

Sometimes elaboration can produce contradictions as in this question asked of housewives:

Which one job about the house do you dread the most— the one you put off just as long as you can?

It is easy to guess that this question worder is himself a putter-offer because he assumes that other people put off the things they dread. Yet some individuals act in just the opposite way and try to get the dreaded things done first. For them, this becomes a contradictory question because of the unnecessary elaboration. It is fully as extreme in one direction as this next question is in the other:

Which part of the cake do you like best—that is, which part do you save for last?

Cat or dog

Just the opposite from the question that talks down or

gets too chummy with the respondent is the approach that tries to confuse or trap him. One such confusing question which made the rounds a few years back was—

Quick! What is Mickey Mouse—a cat or a dog?

Such an outlandish question is not likely to be found in a questionnaire, but it does epitomize the way some of our questions must sound to respondents. The confusing question is more in keeping with courtroom technique than with the voluntary interview situation. Our interviewer should be trying to get the respondent's real thinking down on paper, not trying to thwart and baffle him.

Confusion in questions may be deliberate or not. One that we have already mentioned is the presentation of a card with a deliberately jumbled list of numbers. Numbers usually have a logical arrangement and it is inconsiderate to put them out of order, thus making the respondent's job harder.

Closely allied to the jumbled list of numbers is the list of companies or industries, one or two of which have nothing in common with the rest. The respondent may be asked to assess the employment possibilities in five factories and a bank, for example, or to talk about advancement opportunities in banks, insurance companies, department stores, and coal mines. In each of these cases, one item stands apart from the rest and is so different that it can scarcely be considered with the others. We wouldn't ask, *Which variety of apple ripens latest, or a pear?* Any groupings for comparison should be carefully thought out, whether apples, or pears, or heavy industry, or whatever.

Double negative

Another confusing type may contain a double negative or be unnecessarily complex, leading to the "Yes,-I-mean-no" kind of answer.

Are you against not having prohibition on non-week days, including Sunday and holidays?

A question does not have to have a double negative to be confusing, however. An experiment reported more than thirty years ago indicated that questions which were understood when stated in a clear, positive manner were highly confusing when stated negatively (28). Blankenship reaches the conclusion from reading this experiment that phrasings have a better chance of being understood when expressed positively (6).

Marathon questions

We have already mentioned the difficulty that sometimes may arise when a long and involved statement is followed by "or not." But a lengthy complicated question can in itself be very confusing even though it does state the alternatives. Even in reading it is difficult to get this next one clear the first time. How much harder it must have been to understand it by ear!

What do you think we should do about tariffs and our foreign trade—keep out competition from other countries by raising our tariffs, even if this means we don't have as much foreign trade, or try to increase our trade with other countries by agreeing with them to lower our tariffs if they lower theirs, even if this means some competition from foreign goods?

By any readability score, this marathon question, actually asked in a national survey, would certainly be classified as very difficult. The following chapter in this book is devoted to the importance of brevity and simplicity in avoiding confusion.

This what?

Another source of confusion for some respondents is the confusing antecedent. They may not realize that the questioning is developing along logical lines but think of it as an unrelated series of disjointed questions. It is a source of frequent amazement to the interviewer to have a respondent repeat, "What are my reasons for this?—This what?" immediately after he has answered the directly related question. Yet it happens too often to be ignored.

A safe rule to follow is that unless there is practically no chance of mistaking the antecedent, it is better to repeat it. Don't hesitate to use the same words or phrases over again if it will help to increase understanding.

Why do you feel that way about this?
may be better understood if worded—
Why do you prefer strawberry?

Distinctions without differences

We researchers sometimes become so deeply engrossed in the fine details of our subject matter that we ask two or more questions which sound alike to the respondents. The response, "You just asked me that," is one indication of a poor questionnaire. Efforts on the part of our interviewers to explain the slight distinctions may end in utter confusion.

(1) *What do you like most about Oodles for breakfast?*

(2) *What would you say are the main reasons that you prefer Oodles for breakfast over other kinds of breakfast food?*

Two such questions even though widely separated in the questionnaire may sound strangely alike to the respondent and may cause him to wonder if he understood them both correctly. The researcher who expects somewhat different replies may find that the interviewers did not even bother to ask the second question because it seemed so redundant to them.

Age and birthdate

Some researchers seem to take pleasure in tripping up respondents, outsmarting them, and exposing their inconsistencies. They may ask the same question in two different ways

as, *How old are you?* and *What is the date of your birth?*
They then exult at the supposed concealment of true ages
these questions appear to reveal. In cases of disagreement,
however, either answer may be right. In cases of agreement
it may, of course, be only a reflection of the intelligence of
the respondents and not of their honesty.

You may recall the story of the brilliant child who flunked
her intelligence test. The simple explanation she gave when
confronted with her poor showing was that "silly questions
deserve silly answers."

The smart researcher wants to be sure that in outsmarting
respondents he does not unwittingly outsmart himself. So
beware of questions that are bafflers or thwarters.

Confrontation

Just as there are exceptions to almost every general suggestion made in this book, so we must point out that there
is good reason for certain kinds of confusion techniques. The
repeat interview where specific interest attaches to studying
the consistency of replies affords one such exception. Another
method is very useful in explaining apparent inconsistencies
in the early stages of ballot preparation and testing. A
skilled interviewer can confront the respondent with something like this:

*A few minutes ago you said so-and-so but just now you
said such-and-such. Can you explain why you gave these
answers?*

This type of question is actually an attempt to eliminate
contradiction, inconsistency, and confusion. It can produce
very useful and revealing answers, and may open up new
directions for the research, where at first the respondents
might have seemed to be inconsistent.

For example, the economist may think of independently
established prices as being a necessary part of competition.
Yet, some laymen who agree that there is a great deal of

competition in the oil industry nevertheless think that prices are set in collusion (29). When asked the above type of question, they may explain that all four filling stations on the corner have the same prices but that the proprietors certainly vie with one another to get the trade. We learn from this that substantial parts of the public have a narrow interpretation of competition, but that they are not necessarily inconsistent in their use of it.

Pegs for ideas

When being asked for their general impressions, respondents will sometimes demand some kind of peg on which to hang their ideas. If we ask them, *How about the prices of the things you buy—do prices seem to be higher or lower than they used to be?*, they will ask in return what we mean by *used to be*. Fortunately, in cases like this the flimsiest peg is frequently entirely acceptable to them. In terms of time, for instance, the peg may be as indefinite as—

> *. . . a year or so ago . . .*
> *. . . 15 or 20 years ago . . .*
> *. . . before the war . . .*

In terms of other comparisons, a peg may also be very indefinite—

> *. . . other companies around here . . .*
> *. . . other cities you know about . . .*
> *. . . people like yourself . . .*

Words like "usually," "generally," and "most" are also helpful sometimes in avoiding the quibbling demand of, "What do you mean by that?"

Since pegs are demanded and this demand can so easily be satisfied, it probably is just as well to provide them if doing so is not damaging to the meaning of the general question.

One egg or two?

The interviewer frequently finds it necessary to reassure

prospective respondents that he is not trying to sell them anything. Yet he is in a position where he may "sell" them ideas—influence their replies in one direction or another. The wording of a question can constitute the strongest kind of salesmanship, which of course is usually not desirable in an interview.

One way to increase your awareness of the power of salesmanship is to read *Tested Sentences that Sell* by Elmer Wheeler (30). He is the sell-the-sizzle-not-the-steak man who reports an increase in the sale of eggs in malted milks by having soda jerkers ask, "One egg or two?" instead of, "Would you like an egg in your malted milk?" Examples of this type are excellent salesmanship but poor questionnaire wording. Most of his rules for selling can be preceded with the word "don't" to make them applicable for our particular purposes.

Putting words in the respondent's mouth is one of the worst things we can do, especially when we have obtained the interview in the first place on the basis that we would not try to sell him *anything*.

8. Can you make it brief?

AN ILLUSTRATED LECTURE ON THE VIRTUES OF BREVITY AND SIMPLICITY

THAT questions should be as short as possible and contain only simple words may seem entirely self-evident. This admonishment has probably been stated to question worders more often than any other. Yet little tangible evidence has been presented to show that brevity and simplicity are actually important. Consequently this basic rule may be overlooked too frequently.

The purpose of this chapter is to emphasize by means of concrete illustrations the need for short questions made up of simple words. These examples which have recently been reported in *The Public Opinion Quarterly*, should be a convincing demonstration of the problems associated with lengthy queries and sesquipedalian words (31). But first you will need a briefing on the background and method of the demonstration in order better to understand the examples.

American Petroleum Institute

One of the largest opinion surveys ever made by personal interview was one conducted for the American Petroleum Institute (29). As part of this study, two carefully matched cross sections of the national public, each consisting of about 3,200 persons, were interviewed on two forms of the questionnaire—the split ballot technique again. These two forms were different from each other in only two respects. One of them carried a brief description of the oil industry while the other had no description. The second difference, and the one we are interested in here, is that the statement of alternatives was reversed in sixteen of the questions, thus:

FORM A:

Do you think that this tax is too high, or about right?

FORM B:

Do you think that this tax is about right, or is it too high?

The theory

It was thought that if the order of the alternatives did have any effect, the combination of results from the two wordings would cancel out this effect. But more important from the standpoint of the present discussion, the extent to which respondents were confused by the question might show up in the degree to which the answers varied as the alternatives were transposed.

Under this theory, a "tight" question would be one in which the order of stating the alternatives made no significant difference. For example, the answers to the two variations of the above question came out like this:

	Form A	Form B	Combined
Too high	31%	31%	31%
About right	43	41	42
Too low	1	1	1
No opinion	25	27	26

The differences here are almost negligible. The "too high" choice is taken by the same proportion whether stated first or last, and the "about right" choice increases by 2 percentage points when stated last, making the average difference only 1 per cent in favor of the last alternative. We can say that the order of presenting the alternatives in this question did not affect the answers and that the question is a tight one— not confusing by this test.

On the other hand, the theory is that if reversing the alternatives gives widely differing results, then the question must have some element of confusion, or looseness. None of the sixteen questions proved to be a serious offender on this score, but answers to this next one showed the greatest differences:

FORM A:

Do you think of filling station operators as employees of the oil companies, or as independent businessmen like hardware merchants and lumber dealers who own their own stores?

FORM B:

Do you think of filling station operators as independent businessmen like hardware merchants and lumber dealers who own their own stores, or as employees of the oil companies?

	Form A	Form B	Combined
As employees	29%	37%	33%
As independent businessmen	49	42	46
Qualified answers	15	15	15
No opinion	7	6	6

Thus, under the theory, this question is not a very tight one because reversing the alternatives does affect the replies. When an alternative is presented last, it is chosen by 7% or 8% more respondents than when it is presented first.

Nine tight questions

In the experiment, nine of the sixteen questions turned out to be tight in that differences in results between the two forms did not exceed 2%. These nine tight questions are shown below in only one of the two versions used. Changes in the other version in the two-way questions amounted only to switching the two alternatives about, while in the questions having more than two alternatives the changes amounted to reversing the two extreme alternatives.

Do you think this tax is too high, or about right?

How would you rate the way oil companies treat their dealers—do they give them good treatment, just fair, or poor treatment?

On the whole, how would you say oil companies treat their workers—do they give them good treatment, just fair, or poor treatment?

From what you know or have heard, which would you say gives the customer the most courtesy and attention—grocery stores, drug stores, or filling stations?

Would you say that the present price of gasoline is high, about right, or low in comparison with the prices of other things you buy?

Would you say the price of gasoline, including taxes, has gone up, come down, or stayed the same as it was 15 or 20 years ago?

On the whole, do you think the oil industry makes too much profit, a fair profit, or too little profit?

Do you think there should be more government regulation of the oil industry than there is now, less regulation, or about the same amount?

Would you say this gasoline tax per gallon is higher, lower, or about the same as it was 15 or 20 years ago?

For these nine tight questions, no claim has been made for perfection. The only point to be understood about them is that they have the merit of producing essentially the same results even when the alternatives are reversed. This, of course, might happen sometimes with weak and misunderstood questions, as well as with questions that were entirely clear.

Seven loose ones

We know, however, that something is wrong with the other seven of the sixteen questions because the switching of alternatives there does produce statistically significant differences in replies. These differences range from about 4%

to the 8% in the example already cited. The seven loose questions are:

Do you think of filling station operators as employees of the oil companies, or as independent businessmen like hardware merchants and lumber dealers who own their own stores?

Do you think of the oil industry as being owned by a few large investors, or by thousands of small stockholders?

Well, which of these statements comes closest to your own idea of how gasoline and oil prices are decided: The oil companies get together and set prices for their products, or each company sets its own prices to meet competition?

Some people say that at the rate we are using our oil, it will all be used up in about 15 years. Others say we will still have plenty of oil 100 years from now. Which of these ideas would you guess is most nearly right?

Well, do you think the price has gone up because the price of the gasoline itself has increased, or because taxes have increased, or both?

Is it your impression that there is a great deal of competition between the companies who manufacture and sell gasoline and oil, a medium amount, or only a little competition?

Do you think that oil companies hold back new developments—such as ways for increasing gasoline mileage—or that they are quick to adopt new developments?

The last word

In the first six of these seven loose questions the alternative that appears to be favored is the last one stated. In other words, the alternative appears to be selected more often when it is mentioned last than when it is mentioned first. Perhaps this indicates that respondents tend to remember best the last words they hear. It gives us a third hypothesis about respondent tendencies. You will recall the first two:

[133]

(A) In a list of numbers, those near the middle or in the neighborhood of the average have the greatest drawing power.

(B) In a list of ideas, those at the extremes, particularly at the beginning, have the greatest drawing power.

The third tendency, which may at first seem to contradict the second, is:

(C) In a verbal statement of two ideas, the one stated last has the greater drawing power.

The exception

Answers to the seventh loose question, however, indicate that in this one case the alternative stated first has the greater drawing power. But this may be a very special case. It might be conjectured that respondents tend to answer it early, even before they hear the second alternative. The punctuation does appear especially conducive to this possibility, since the pauses indicated by the dashes might have caused some respondents to jump the gun. More about this later in Chapter 12.

Do you think the oil companies are quick to adopt new developments—such as ways for increasing gasoline mileage—or that they hold back new developments?

Another possibility is that because the example, "ways of increasing gasoline mileage," goes with whichever alternative comes first, respondents tended to grab it as a handle in making their decisions. Without direct evidence on these points it is necessary to withhold judgment as to whether this question is an exception or whether it is a special case that does not come under the general hypothesis that the last alternative has the preferred position.

Concept words

Cursory inspection of the two sets of questions gives the

impression that the seven loose questions are generally more complex than are the nine tight questions. This impression is correct as we will soon see. Still, it is only in certain respects that the loose questions are more complex than the others. For example, the loose questions contain no more concept words (independent, investors, competition, developments, etc.) than do the tight ones (treatment, attention, profit, regulation, etc.). While the use of vague concept words is something we should try to avoid if we can, it seems that the differences between the two groups of questions cannot be ascribed to this feature.

No opinion answers

It is generally conceded that phrasing can sway opinions most easily when those opinions are not strongly held. But there is no evidence that the strength of opinions on the loose questions was any less than on the tight questions. Quite the contrary, the no opinion answers themselves on the seven loose questions averaged only 9 per cent as compared with 18 per cent on the nine tight questions. Even if we include the middle ground answers (qualified, in between, about the same, etc.) with the no opinion answers, the total averages 21 per cent for the loose questions as against 27% for the tight ones. These findings would lead to the paradoxical idea that opinions were less strongly held on the tight questions than on the loose ones.

So it is probably neither concept words nor weak opinions that cause the looseness of the loose questions here.

Number of words

We can get closer to the telling differences between the two groups of questions by counting the number of words in each. The longest of the tight questions has 26 words while the shortest contains only 11 words. Against this, the length of the loose questions ranges from 21 to 46 words.

On the average, the loose questions are one and a half times as long as the tight ones—31 words to 22 words.

If we count only the words used in expressing the alternatives, that is excluding the introductory or stage-setting phrases, we find that this same ratio holds. The statement of the alternatives in the loose questions is one and a half times as long as in the tight ones.

Therefore, it seems clear that one element of tightness in a question is brevity. For a not too difficult goal, we might try to keep our questions somewhere in the neighborhood of 20 words or less.

Difficult words

Another difference between the two groups of questions is found in the ratio of difficult words to total words. For example, one word in every eight in the loose questions, but only one in every twelve in the tight questions, has more than two syllables.

Count of the number of affixes (prefixes and suffixes) per 100 words shows much the same situation. The loose questions average more than 40 affixes to 100 words, while the tight questions average fewer than 30.

Thus we find not only that the loose questions tend to be longer than the others, but also that they are usually stated in more difficult terms. This illustrates the need for simplicity as well as brevity.

Flesch Scores

In his book, *The Art of Plain Talk*, Rudolf Flesch outlined a method of scoring the readability of written material (32). He computed his scores from average sentence length, number of affixes in 100 words, and average number of personal references in 100 words. His scoring method is intended for use on straight reading matter and not for isolated questions given verbally. But we may apply his method to survey questions if we keep in mind that using his score gives such questions every benefit of the doubt from the standpoint of their being stated in terms which would hold respondent interest. For one thing, Flesch says that written communication can be pitched higher than oral communication, because the written word is easier to follow than the spoken word. It seems evident also that a sentence is easier to understand in context within a written article than is a question asked in a more or less isolated situation.

According to the Flesch method, the nine tight questions qualify as "standard," or suitable as reading material for people who have completed the seventh or eighth grade. The seven loose questions are rated "difficult" or suited for the reading of people who have completed high school or some college. Flesch says, in contrast, that "very easy reading" consists of sentences averaging eight words or less with fewer than two affixes a sentence. This style of writing appeals to a potential audience of fourth-grade attainments.

We should note that Flesch does not imply that more difficult reading matter cannot be comprehended by people of low educational attainments. His scoring device takes into account only what people at different levels will be likely to read with interest. Possibly the saving grace in many a long complex survey question is that understanding of it extends more widely than does any reader appeal it might have.

Whatever the interpretation we read into the Flesch scores, however, it seems evident that we should set our sights much lower in terms of brevity and simplicity if we are to avoid overshooting the target. Fay Terris comes to the same conclusion after subjecting 144 survey questions from three different polling organizations to the Flesch formula (33).

9. What's the good word?

A FUTILE SEARCH FOR A LIST OF PERFECT
WORDS, SUPPLEMENTED BY A LIST OF 1,000
WELL-KNOWN WORDS

At the end of this chapter you will find a list of words, which in a book like this you might guess to be an endorsed and approved list for question wording. Before you jump to that happy but unwarranted assumption, I earnestly urge that you read the preliminary discussion.

Most question worders, myself included, would welcome a list of "good" words—words that could without question be used in any question. Essentially, these words should be both single in meaning and generally understood. "Almost," "because," and "I" are good examples. All three are in frequent use, all are readily recognized by fourth-grade children, and each has but a single meaning.

But the list of words which would fulfill all these requirements would not be very long. Familiarity, wide usage, and single meanings do not go hand in hand. Quite the contrary, words that come into common use tend in the process to acquire a variety of meanings and nuances. We seldom consult the dictionary about these well-known words. Yet they are the ones which usually have the greatest flexibility of meaning. Take "run" for example. Your own desk dictionary doubtless shows more than 50 meanings of this word!

When a new word is put into use, it is usually because existing words are inadequate or are not specific enough to convey the particular meaning desired. So we are continually coining new and unambiguous words, but these words are unfamiliar to most people. Thus, the natural development of language tends to go against our search for a list of "good" words. The familiar words have too many meanings and the words of single meaning are not well known.

Of course, the search for the words to use in one particular question is not so futile as is the compilation of a list of words that could be relied upon for use in all questions. For one thing, a word of many meanings may have only the one desired meaning when placed in context with the rest of the question. For another, the meanings may be so closely related that they all add up to practically the same thing so far as that particular question goes. Yet we couldn't list such words as being always satisfactory because questions with other contexts might allow the ambiguities to slip in. So, we can never expect to see a very long list of fully endorsed words.

Basic English

As question worders, we can learn something important from Basic English, even though it does not provide the particular list of words we need. Basic English is English made simple by reducing the number of its words to 850 and by reducing the number of rules for using them to a minimum. Its originators claim that with these words, their derivatives, conjugations, plurals, etc., it is possible to say anything needed for the general purposes of everyday living. They include talking about business, trade, industry, science, medical work, all the arts of living and all the exchanges of knowledge, desires, beliefs, opinions, and news which are the chief work of a language. They make a pretty good case for their claim, too (34).

Therein lies the lesson we can gain from Basic. It is really not necessary to employ a tremendous vocabulary in talking of the things which most people are likely to be able to discuss with us. If we find that we have to use highly particularized or unfamiliar words, perhaps we should ask ourselves whether we aren't exploring an issue that is beyond the likelihood of general public comprehension. Stuart Chase conjectures that "more than half of the questions asked by accredited pollsters since 1936 should probably never have been attempted" (35).

Let's keep in the front of our thinking the fact that it is possible to express almost anything we may have need to with only 850 basic words. This fact will give us something to aim for when we are inclined to let some abstruse or unfamiliar term slip by merely because we can't immediately think of any other way of expressing it. If we really try, we can probably bring it down at least to the level of a 2000-word vocabulary.

Why, then, isn't Basic English just the list of words we need? The main reason is that insufficient numbers of people have adopted this simplified language. It sounds like English, and, in fact, is English—but with certain qualifications which make it not so familiar to our ears as it might be. For example, in Basic you may "do an addition" instead of "adding." Each word of Basic has been carefully selected as being the best of existing English words for expressing a certain central meaning. But such words are not necessarily the most familiar ones. Clearly, "instrument" is a useful word, but fourth-grade children are more familiar with the separate names of many different instruments than they are with this master word.

In summary, we can hope to do a better job of wording questions if we don't confine ourselves to Basic English. But Basic's ability to express almost anything with only 850 words should goad us into seriously trying to use as few unfamiliar words as possible in our questions.

Dictionary

Now for a further constructive approach to the selection of words for a question. Let us assume that we have already stated the issue as precisely as we can but without much regard for its understandability. Our next thought is to turn to the dictionary to see whether the question may be restated more directly and more simply. We can look up each word, asking these six questions about it:

(1) Does it mean what we intend?

(2) Does it have any other meanings?

(3) If so, does the context make the intended meaning clear?

(4) Does the word have more than one pronunciation?

(5) Is there any word of similar pronunciation that might be confused?

(6) Is a simpler word or phrase suggested (either in the dictionary or in a thesaurus)?

Of course, it is possible that our original statement happens to be made up entirely of words that fulfill the requirements. Then, as far as the dictionary is concerned, the statement up to this point is satisfactory and there is still no need to change it. If as written it conveys the precise meaning intended and has no element of confusion, we have done a good job so far as the dictionary can tell us.

I say "so far as the dictionary can tell us" because the dictionary is far from being the last word in solving problems of communication. Its definitions are just too definite, too literal, too formalized, to give any feeling or value to the words.

Good, fair, poor

For an example of the use of the dictionary, we might try looking up the word "fair" for the frequently used question context of "good, fair, or poor." We are looking for a colorless, middle-ground word which neither commends nor condemns and, sure enough, "fair" has the adjective meaning of "average." We see right away, however, that it also has many other meanings. We can discount those where it is used as a noun—"county fair," etc—and as light or clear, because the context clearly rules out such meanings. But some of the other adjective meanings edge nearer to possible misinterpretation: "Just, honest, according to the rules, pretty good, not bad, favorable, beautiful, courteous, clean, plain, open, and seeming good at first but not really so."

Even when the results of a good-fair-poor question have been received, equally competent analysts sometimes argue whether the "fair" group leans more to the "good" side as in the "pretty good" definition or the "bad" side as in the "seeming good, but not" idea. That is, in the interpretation are "fair" responses to be considered as "pretty good" or discounted as "only fair"? This argument may seem foolish, but it has taken place and it does serve to emphasize the weakness in this word.

To go on with the dictionary, the fact that "fair" has only one pronunciation is a point in its favor. At least, it would not be a stumbling block for interviewers as might be the double pronunciations of "lead" and "wind" in this hypothetical question to be asked of fishermen:

How much lead do you use on your sinker when you have a good wind?

True, there is another word of like pronunciation, "fare." But this other word, always used as a noun or verb, is not at all likely to create confusion in this context.

Evidently, then, "fair" is satisfactory on some scores, but it has enough faults that we should try to find a substitute. Among the possible replacements for "fair" are these:

average	middle	ordinary
between	moderate	standard
indifferent	neutral	usual
medium	normal	

But several of these words are subject to much the same variability we are trying to avoid in the word "fair." "Indifferent," "ordinary," and "usual" all sometimes carry a somewhat below average stigma. "Standard" may imply excellence, while "normal" seems to have more of a good than a bad connotation. "Middle" taken literally may be too specific a term in the sense of *exactly halfway between*.

In making such judgments as these, I am on shaky ground, of course. One might question, for instance, my ruling out "middle" on the basis of literal definition but leaving in "medium" which itself is defined as "having a middle position." Most of these words are defined in terms of one another anyway, which is part of what I meant when I said the dictionary is not the last word in the choice of words. If we take it too literally, we find ourselves going round and round the cobbler's bench, only to end up where we started. It happens that to me "medium" appears to be not so subject to the over-specific problem as "middle" is, but I could easily be wrong.

In the dictionary on my desk (36) the remaining five words have from four to nine meanings each, as compared with the eighteen meanings of "fair." The only one which has more than three meanings as an adjective, however, is "neutral" with seven adjectival meanings. Eliminating it leaves us with four possible candidates:

average	medium
between	moderate

These are all rather colorless words so that it may seem to be a toss-up among them. In any case, the dictionary can't take us much farther than this in selecting our intermediate word for our "good, ———, poor."

Lorge magazine count

From a count of words as they actually appear in print we can gain a good idea of which are the most popular. Irving Lorge in *The Teacher's Word Book of 30,000 Words* reports how often each word appeared in a count of 4,500,000 words in popular magazines (37). He used the *Saturday Evening*

Post, Woman's Home Companion, Ladies' Home Journal, True Story, and *Reader's Digest*, taking twelve issues of each spread over the years 1927 through 1938.

For our purposes, this Lorge magazine count is probably the best of the several word counts that have been published. It is comparatively current, whereas some of the other counts have a high representation of so-called ageless literature. The Lorge count comes from popular writing rather than from classics or "good literature." It is not based on reading matter selected for any particular group such as high-school students.

You may be interested to see that these twelve words make up more than 25 per cent of all the words that appeared in the five magazines:

the	to	in	it
and	of	was	he
a	I	that	you

That is, in the 4,500,000 words that were counted, these twelve simple words occurred a total of 1,143,422 times!

Back to the middle-ground words which we have under consideration, here are the frequencies with which they occurred in the four-and-a-half-million count:

between	1,526	times
fair	561	times
average	519	times
medium	119	times
moderate	109	times

So far, then, "between" seems to be the best of the middle-ground possibilities: It is popular, it has the desired meaning, and only the one meaning in this context.

In terms of frequency, "moderate" and "medium" would be the least desirable of the five words. The exclusion of these two words illustrates the chief use of the word count.

It is a negative use—namely, to point out the words of low frequency so that we may substitute more popular terms for them.

The converse does not work so well—a word of high frequency is not always a good one to use. For one thing, it may not have high frequency in the particular meaning we intend to convey. Even different words that are spelled alike may have been counted together. Thus, "wind" appears only once, even though different pronunciations of the "i" make it actually two different words. In effect, the counts for two words are thereby combined in this instance. For another thing, the word of high frequency is likely to have a variety of different meanings.

Another caution about the use of word counts has to do with compound words. The fact that each of two words has high frequency does not mean that a combination of the two will have high frequency. The idea of "public opinion" is not a very common idea although "public" had a count of 1047 and "opinion" a count of 438. Furthermore, the concept we have of "public opinion" is not clearly apparent from the separate descriptions of the two words in a dictionary.

So the word count taken alone is not a sufficient guide for the selection of words. It is useful for the elimination of low-frequency words, but affords no guarantee of perfection in high-frequency words.

Dale list

Edgar Dale of Ohio State University has compiled a different kind of word list (38). It is made up of 3,000 words that are known in reading to four in every five children in the fourth grade. Almost all of the first thousand most-used words according to the Lorge magazine count appear also in the Dale list. However, the Dale list naturally includes a number of childish words like "baa," "boo," and "elf," which are very far down in the word count.

If we consider that people of fourth-grade attainments approximate the lowest level of the population to be included in a survey, the Dale list becomes a valuable aid for question wording. Again, this is in the negative sense that words excluded from his list are suspect—not in the positive sense that all words on the list could be considered simon-pure. Also, the Dale list, like the magazine count, is based on written instead of oral communication, a fact which scarcely makes it the best criterion for verbal questions.

The Dale list was presented primarily as giving "a significant correlation with reading difficulty. It includes words that are unimportant and excludes some important ones. To use the list for more than an overall statistical device which gives a good prediction of readability would be out of harmony with the purpose for which it was constructed."

Despite this caution suggested by the authors of the original articles on the Dale list, we must do with that list and the Lorge magazine count until something more directly applicable to the wording of verbal questions comes along. Until then, we must keep in mind that there is no reliable list of "good" words, that words on these lists are not guaranteed as unambiguous, but that words off the lists are suspect of being unfamiliar. Any value the lists have must be included within these very hazy limits.

Good, poor, or in between

The only two of our four middle-ground words that appear on the Dale list are "between" and "fair." This brings us around to "between" as the best prospect, since dissatisfaction with "fair" started us out on the search in the first place. We can word the alternatives as "good, poor, or between" or "good, poor, or in between" with some assurance that the middle-ground choice will be familiar to practically everyone, clearly understood, and practically colorless.

If all this seems like going through a lot of motions for the statement of a single idea, we have three consolations. First, we recall that just twelve words make up at least a fourth of all those we are likely to use. Once we have analyzed these twelve words and found their weaknesses, we won't have to check every time we need to use them. We can probably extend this experience to cover several hundred of the most commonly used words, so that after our first few questionnaires, we may have to look up only every fifth or every tenth word in a proposed question.

The second consoling feature is that this approach to the selection of words reduces the necessity of relying on the pretest to uncover double meanings. Why should we wait until a test interviewer reports that certain persons misunderstand what we are talking about? By careful study, we can probably eliminate that confusion in advance and perhaps also some other sources of confusion that the test interviews don't bring to light.

And finally, this procedure enables us to direct the pretesting toward the problem words. Frequently, we may have to use a word that might be ambiguous according to the dictionary or unfamiliar according to the word lists. This procedure points out such words so that we can tag them for the test interviewer. Are they actually ambiguous? Are they really unrecognized?

By the use of dictionary, Lorge magazine count, and Dale list, we at once simplify and sharpen the test interview. We remove the needless clutter of ambiguous and unfamiliar words and we point out the remaining possible sources of difficulty. It is true that the question worder has to work harder, but the test interviewer works better, and the end result should be an improvement in questions.

"Good average"

Incidentally, now that its absence from the Dale list has eliminated "average" along with some of the other possible substitutes, you may be interested to see this difficult-to-classify answer:

Would you say that Podunk is a good, average, or poor place to live?

"Oh, I'd say it's a good average place to live."

This combination reply is something that would not be anticipated from a dictionary or any other source. It illustrates one need for pretesting even when a question has been very carefully devised in other respects.

Words, just words

On the next few pages is an alphabetical list of 1,000 words, all familiar and all in frequent use. We have talked about the Lorge magazine count and the Dale list. This is a combination of the two. The words shown here are the ones on the Dale list which appear in the Lorge magazine count more than 402 times. These are not to be taken as "good" words, but only as familiar and popular words. Some of them, in fact, are designated as problem words. All these words are known to fourth-grade children and all are included among the most frequently used words in popular magazines.

It happens that this list includes almost all the workaday words of the curious—all the *how, who, what, which, why, when,* and *where*'s that are associated with our business. It has many of the alternatives we have to use: *for* and *against, big* and *little, large* and *small, good* and *bad, black* and *white, same* and *different.* Even if we never pay much attention to this list, we shall be using most of its words over and over again.

Now, to mention some of the things we can learn from this list.

Three syllables?

Naturally, we should expect words on our list to be simple. And they are. Only 6 per cent of them have as many as three syllables, for example. Now, no grudge should be held against a polysyllabic word just because it has so many syllables. "Electricity" may be better known and understood than "watt." "Hospitalization insurance" may be more widely understood than a clumsy circumlocution of short words devised to take its place.

But since so few long words enjoy familiarity and wide usage, perhaps we can afford to be critical of them. Whenever we feel the need to use a word of more than two syllables, let's draw a circle around it to bring it to the tester's special attention.

Blab words

Also, you cannot help noting that our list has very few concept words like "art," "business," and "government." This is just as well. Such words, because they are so general, are seldom very useful in questions. They are the kind that require definition or specific modifiers if they are to be meaningful. Otherwise, whose concept is to be accepted—yours, mine, his, hers?

In the realm of exploring general concepts, we question worders probably make our biggest mistakes. Too often we take for granted that the respondent's idea of the idea is the same as our own idea of the idea. Then we say that the public thinks such and such of this idea. Maybe the whole idea of asking about the idea was wrong in the first place.

Stuart Chase in *The Tyranny of Words* suggests that we might as well say "blab" when we use a high-order abstraction so far as conveying a clear meaning is concerned (39). Some words have so many overtones and emotional qualifications that their original meanings are frequently lost sight of. Some are so indefinite that they have no concrete referents and therefore are meaningless. Here is a typical blab-blab question:

(blab)   (blab)   (blab)

Should our country be more active in world affairs?

What is conveyed by the word "country" in this instance— our government as a whole, the State Department, our commercial firms, our industrialists, or what?

"More active?" In what way? How active is our country now?

"World affairs?" Oh, brother!

These are the kind of terms that have to be defined explicitly before philosophers can begin to discuss them. Let's not inflict them on the general public with no definitions whatever! That is, let's not do it unless we have some follow-up questions which enable us to realize the multitude of combinations or frames of reference such blab words bring up.

* and †

Two types of marks appear with some of the words on our list. These marks indicate words which for one or another reason are most likely to cause trouble in our questions. The * in front of a word signifies that someone has had an experience or a bit of special knowledge about that word which would sometimes make it a problem word. One in every twelve words on the list is thus designated as a problem word. In the next chapter I shall try to explain the difficulty with each of these words.

The † in front of a word indicates that the word has 10 or more meanings in the *Thorndike Century Senior Dictionary*. Such words in particular may need to be looked up—not that there is any merit in the arbitrary choice of 10 as a dividing line.

It happens that about a third of the words in the list carry the † mark. This fact should emphasize the need for frequent reference to the dictionary. The same rule of ten applied to *Webster's Unabridged* or the *American College Dictionary* would result in the marking of even more words.

The fact that a word carries neither mark does not necessarily indicate that it is a "good" word. The absence of such notations means only that the word hasn't so far distinguished itself as a problem word and that it has fewer than 10 meanings in *Thorndike*. Some of these meanings may make it ambiguous, or it may be a problem word on some other score than meaning. Notice that many words carry the * without the †. Even with fewer than 10 meanings, these words have proved themselves to be problem words.

The general idea, then, is that we should consider every word with caution and those having † and * with even more caution.

Derivatives

In addition to the words actually appearing on our list, it is reasonable, of course, to consider their simple derivatives as being in the same category. Regular plurals and possessives of the nouns, simple forms of the verbs, comparatives and superlatives of the adjectives, all may be taken as though they were on the list themselves. Also, common contractions such as "don't," "can't," and "he's" are left off the list only because they would unnecessarily add to its length.

1000 FREQUENT-FAMILIAR WORDS

a	add	ago	along
able	address	agree	already
*†about	afraid	ahead	also
above	†after	air	*always
accept	afternoon	*†all	am
account	again	allow	*America
across	against	almost	*American
†act	age	alone	among

* Problem word.   † Multi-meaning word.

amount	beg	building	†clear
an	began	built	climb
*and	begin	†burn	†close
another	†behind	*business	clothes
answer	being	busy	club
*any	*believe	but	coat
*anybody	belong	butter	coffee
*anyone	below	buy	cold
*anything	beside	†by	college
*anyway	besides		†color
apartment	*best	cabin	colored
appear	better	cake	†come
are	between	†call	comfort
arm	big	†came	coming
†around	†bill	†camp	company
arrange	†bit	†can	cook
arrive	†black	cannot	†cool
*†art	†blind	captain	†corner
†as	blood	car	cost
ask	blue	card	cotton
†at	†board	care	*could
attention	boat	†carry	†count
aunt	bob	†case	*country
automobile	†body	†catch	†course
away	boil	caught	†court
	†book	cause	†cover
baby	born	cent	crazy
†back	both	†center	†cream
*bad	bought	certain	†cross
bag	†box	certainly	crowd
bake	boy	chair	†cry
†ball	bread	chance	†cup
†bank	break	†change	curtain
be	breakfast	†charge	†cut
†bear	breath	†check	
†beat	bridge	cheek	dad
beautiful	bright	chief	*daily
beauty	bring	child	†dance
became	†broke	children	dare
because	†broken	Christmas	†dark
become	brother	church	daughter
†bed	brought	city	day
been	brown	†class	†dead
before	†brush	†clean	†deal

---

* Problem word.   † Multi-meaning word.

[152]

dear	egg	fifty	†gather
death	eight	fight	gave
decide	either	†figure	gay
†deep	else	fill	†general
desire	end	finally	gentleman
desk	enemy	†find	*†get
†did	English	†fine	girl
die	enjoy	finger	*give
difference	enough	finish	†given
different	enter	†fire	glad
*dinner	escape	first	glance
†direct	†even	fish	glass
direction	evening	†fit	*†go
discover	*ever	five	going
dish	*every	†flat	†goes
†do	*everybody	floor	god
doctor	*everything	flower	gold
†does	except	†fly	golden
dog	expect	†follow	†gone
dollar	explain	following	†good
†done	†eye	food	†got
door		fool	*government
†down	†face	†foot	grand
dozen	fact	†for	gray
†draw	fail	forget	great
dream	*†fair	forgotten	†green
†dress	faith	†form	grew
†drew	†fall	forth	†ground
drink	family	forward	group
†drive	far	†found	grow
†drop	farm	four	†guard
†drove	fashion	†free	guess
*†dry	†fast	French	guest
due	†fat	†fresh	gun
during	†father	friend	
duty	fear	from	habit
	†feel	†front	†had
*each	feet	fruit	hair
ear	†fell	†full	half
early	†fellow	fun	hall
earth	†felt	funny	†hand
†easy	*few	further	happen
eat	†field		happiness
edge	fifteen	garden	happy

* Problem word. † Multi-meaning word.

[153]

†hard	idea	†last	*†make
†has	if	late	man
hat	important	laugh	manager
hate	impossible	*†law	many
*†have	†in	lawyer	†march
he	inch	†lay	†mark
†head	indeed	†lead	†market
health	Indian	lean	marriage
*hear	inside	learn	married
*heard	instead	least	marry
†heart	interesting	†leave	†match
†heat	into	†led	†matter
heaven	†iron	left	may
†heavy	is	leg	maybe
†held	*it	*less	me
†help	*its	†let	meal
her	itself	†letter	†mean
here		library	meant
herself	†job	lie	meat
†high	join	†life	†meet
him	joy	†lift	meeting
himself	judge	†light	member
his	juice	*†like	men
history	†jump	†line	†met
†hit	June	lip	middle
†hold	*†just	†list	*might
†home		listen	mile
hope	†keep	little	milk
†horse	†kept	†live	million
hospital	kid	living	†mind
hot	†kill	long	†mine
hotel	kind	look	minute
hour	kiss	†lose	miss
†house	kitchen	†lost	mistake
how	knee	†lot	moment
however	*knew	†love	money
hundred	*know	lovely	month
†hung	known	†low	*more
hurry		lunch	morning
hurt	lady		*most
husband	†laid	machine	†mother
	lake	†made	motor
I	†land	magazine	mouth
†ice	large	mail	†move

---

* Problem word.   † Multi-meaning word.

[154]

Mr.	oil	†plant	really
Mrs.	†old	†play	reason
*much	†on	pleasant	†receive
music	once	please	†record
must	†one	pleasure	red
my	*only	plenty	refuse
myself	†open	†pocket	remain
	*or	†point	remember
†name	†order	police	remove
*†near	other	*poor	†repeat
nearly	ought	*possible	†report
neck	our	†post	†rest
need	ourselves	†pound	†return
neither	†out	pour	rich
*never	†outside	powder	†ride
†new	†over	†power	†right
news	*own	prepare	†ring
newspaper		†present	†rise
next		pretty	river
†nice	†pack	price	road
night	page	†print	†rock
nine	†paid	promise	†roll
no	pain	proud	roof
*nobody	paint	prove	room
nod	pale	*public	†rose
*none	†paper	†pull	†round
nor	parent	†push	†rule
†nose	park	*†put	†run
not	†part		†rush
†note	party		
*nothing	†pass	question	safe
notice	†past	†quickly	said
*†now	†pay	quiet	salad
†number	peace	*quite	sale
†nurse	*people		†salt
	perhaps	†race	same
o'clock	person	†raise	†sat
†of	†pick	†ran	Saturday
†off	picture	rather	†save
offer	†piece	†reach	*†saw
office	†place	*†read	say
officer	†plain	reader	†school
often	plan	ready	sea
oh	†plane	real	

---

* Problem word.   † Multi-meaning word.

[155]

search	†sing	stair	†taken
†season	†single	†stand	†talk
†seat	sir	†star	tall
†second	sister	stare	†taste
secret	†sit	†start	tea
*†see	six	†state	†tear
seem	size	station	teeth
*†seen	†skin	†stay	telephone
sell	sleep	†step	†tell
send	†slip	†stick	ten
sense	†slow	†still	†term
sent	slowly	†stir	terrible
†serve	†small	†stock	test
*†service	†smart	†stood	than
†set	smile	†stop	thank
†settle	†smoke	store	*†that
seven	†so	story	*the
*several	†soft	†straight	theater
†shade	sold	strange	their
†shadow	†some	street	them
shall	somebody	†stretch	then
†shape	someone	†strong	there
share	something	†study	*these
she	*sometimes	†stuff	they
†ship	somewhere	†subject	†thick
shoe	son	*such	†thin
†shook	soon	sudden	thing
shop	sorry	suffer	think
†short	sort	sugar	third
†shot	soul	†suit	*this
*should	†sound	summer	*those
shoulder	†space	sun	though
shout	†speak	Sunday	thought
†show	spend	*supper	thousand
shut	spent	suppose	three
†sick	†spirit	*sure	throat
†side	†spoke	surely	through
†sight	†sport	surprise	ticket
*†sign	spot	sweet	†tie
silence	†spread		till
silent	†spring	†table	†time
†simple	†square	tablespoon	tiny
since	†stage	*†take	tired

* Problem word.   † Multi-meaning word.

†to	†under	wedding	woman
*today	understand	week	women
together	unless	†well	wonder
†told	until	†went	wonderful
tomorrow	†up	were	†wood
†tone	†upon	west	†word
tonight	us	what	†work
*too	†use	when	worker
†took		*†where	world
†top	vegetable	which	worry
†touch	very	while	worse
toward	view	whisper	worth
*town	visit	†white	would
trade	†voice	*who	write
†train		whole	written
†tree	wait	whom	wrong
†tried	†walk	whose	wrote
*†trip	wall	why	
trouble	want	†wide	yard
†true	war	wife	year
†trust	†warm	†wild	yellow
truth	was	†will	yes
†try	†wash	†wind	yet
†turn	†watch	window	*you
twelve	†water	winter	young
twenty	†wave	wire	your
twice	†way	wise	yourself
two	we	wish	youth
	†wear	†with	
uncle	weather	without	

* Problem word.   † Multi-meaning word.

10. What's wrong with "you"?

A ROGUE'S GALLERY OF PROBLEM WORDS, WITH CASE HISTORIES

IN THIS chapter we shall concentrate our attention on the "problem" words which were just now pointed out in our list—the words designated by the *. The problems associated with these words are not all alike. Some are difficulties with the words themselves. Others result from the situations in which the particular words may be used. Some of the problems are perfectly obvious and hardly need mentioning except to make the record complete.

Other problems described here may seem far-fetched and ridiculous, and perhaps some of them are. Still, although a particular word may be all right in 99 questions out of 100, it may create a serious problem in that hundredth question. It is just this type of word which probably most needs to be discussed.

Even *you

Let's talk about "you" for a while. We've discussed how some words of high frequency also have numerous meanings. Here is a word that has high frequency and almost singleness of meaning. But even something as good as "you" may sometimes be bad.

"You" is extremely popular with question worders, being implicated in every question we ask. And, question wording aside, "you" ranks twelfth in frequency of use according to the Lorge magazine count. On the average, this word appears once in every hundred words printed in popular magazines. (Parenthetically and of no particular importance to this discussion, "I" happens to appear twice as often—a commentary on something or other.)

The dictionary distinguishes only two or three meanings of "you"—the second person singular and plural and the substitution for the impersonal "one"—"How do you get there?" in place of "How does one get there?" In most questions "you" gives no trouble whatever, it being clear that we are asking the opinion of the second person singular. However, and here is the problem, the word sometimes may have a collective meaning as in a question asked of radio repairmen:

How many radio sets did you repair last month?
This question seemed to work all right until one repairman in a large shop countered with, "Who do you mean, me or the whole shop?"

Much as we might want to, therefore, we can't give "you" an unqualified recommendation. Sometimes "you" needs the emphasis of "you yourself" and sometimes it just isn't the word to use, as in the above situation where the entire shop was meant.

*about

Among other uses, "about" is sometimes intended to mean somewhere near in the sense that both 48% and 52% are "about" half. It is also used to mean nearly or almost, in the sense that 48% is "about" half while 52% is "over" half. This small difference in interpretation may make a slight difference in the way various respondents answer certain questions.

*all

Here is the first mention of a "dead giveaway" word, a term you will see frequently from here on.

Your own experience with true-false tests has probably demonstrated to you that it is safe to count almost every all-inclusive statement as false. That is, you have learned in such tests that it is safe to follow the idea that "all statements containing 'all' are false, including this one." Some people have the same negative reaction to opinion questions which hinge upon all-inclusive or all-exclusive words. They may be generally in agreement with a proposition, but nevertheless hesitate to accept the extreme idea of *all, always, each, every, never, nobody, only, none,* or *sure.*

> *Would you say that all cats have four legs?*
> *Is the mayor doing all he can for the city?*

It is correct, of course, to use an all-inclusive word if it correctly states the alternative. But you will usually find that such a word produces an overstatement. Most people may go along with the idea, accepting it as a form of literary license, but the purists and quibblers may either refuse to give an opinion or may even choose the other side in protest.

*always

This is another dead giveaway word.

> *Do you always observe traffic signs?*
> *Is your boss always friendly?*

*America

*American

Be careful of two things with words like these. First, they may be heavily loaded emotional concepts. Answers may be given in terms of patriotism instead of the issue at hand. Second, these are very indefinite words referring to whole continents or parts of continents, to Indians or even to that sometimes misused phrase—100% Americans.

*and

This simple conjunction in some contexts may be taken either as separating two alternatives or as connecting two parts of a single alternative.

> *Is there much rivalry among the boys who sell soda pop and crackerjack?*

[160]

Some people will answer in terms of rivalry between two groups—those who sell pop and those who sell crackerjack. Others will take it as rivalry within the single group comprising both pop and crackerjack salesmen.

*any

The trouble with this word is a bit difficult to explain. It's something like that optical illusion of the shifting stairsteps, which you sometimes seem to see from underneath and sometimes seem to see from above but which you aren't able to see both ways at the same time. The trouble with "any" is that it may mean "every," "some," or "one only" in the same sentence or question, depending on the way you look at it.

See whether you can get both the "every" and "only one" illusions from this question and notice the difference in meaning that results:

Do you think any word is better than the one we are discussing?

You could think, "Yes, I think just any old word (every word) is better." On the other hand, you might think, "Yes, I believe it would be possible to find a better word."

Another difficulty with "any" is that when used in either the "every" or the "not any" context it becomes as much a dead giveaway word as are "every" and "none."

*anybody

Words with the "any" root are subject to the same trouble as "any" itself. "Anybody" can mean everybody or some one person.

Do you think that anybody could do this job?

"Sure, it's so simple that anyone could do it."

"Yes, probably Paul Bunyan could."

*anyone

This dead giveaway word may mean everyone or a certain one.

*anything

Everything or one particular thing?

*anyway

By now perhaps you see how difficult it is for anybody to understand anything clearly from these any-words anyway.

*art

This is a concept word if ever there was one. If it had a clear, definite meaning, then there would be no need for philosophical debates on such issues as—

Is question wording an art or a science?

*bad

In itself the word "bad" is not at all bad for question wording. It conveys the meaning desired and is satisfactory as an alternative in a "good or bad" two-way question.

Experience seems to indicate, however, that people are generally less willing to criticize than they are to praise. Since it is difficult to get them to state their negative views, sometimes the critical side needs to be softened. For example, after asking, *What things are good about your job?*, it might seem perfectly natural to ask, *What things are bad about it?* But if we want to lean over backwards to get as many criticisms as we can, we may be wise not to apply the "bad" stigma but to ask, *What things are not so good about it?*

*believe

This sometimes has stronger connotations than "think" or "suppose" and therefore should not be used as a substitute for them. A person may think a certain thing without believing it.

Which horse do you think will win the Derby?
Which horse do you believe will win the Derby?

[162]

*best

In some applications, this is a dead giveaway word. Few people do the *best* they can, for example.

*business

This has sometimes been interpreted as "busy-ness." "Business" is one of the concept words mentioned earlier. Although questions often center around business as an individual company, as a group of companies, or as the entire trade, we have no adequate term or terms to describe these several concepts. In this case I point to the fact that the word is unsatisfactory, with little hope of ever finding a better term.

*could

No fault is found with the word itself, but we are well advised to remember that it should not be confused with "should" or "might."

*country

What is meant by this word—the nation as a whole, or rural areas?

*daily

Which is intended—six days a week, or all seven?

*dinner

Dinner, the main meal of the day, comes at noon with some families and in some areas. Elsewhere it is the evening meal. The question should not assume that it is either the one or the other.

*dry

In prohibition studies, it has actually happened that some people have thought we were asking about the weather when we discussed the Wet-Dry issue.

*each

Sometimes, when used in the "every" sense, this is a dead giveaway word.

*ever

This word tends to be a dead giveaway in a very special sense. "Ever" is such a long time and so inclusive that it makes it seem plausible that some unimpressive things may have happened.

Have you ever listened to the Song Plugger radio program?

"Yes—I suppose I must have at some time or other."

*every

Another dead giveaway. Putting forth *every* effort is pretty extreme, for example.

*everybody

Another one. "Everybody" includes billions of people.

*everything

And another.

*fair

This word was discussed at length in the "good, fair, poor" context in Chapter 9. Also, when used in the sense of "just" or "reasonable" it sometimes may be taken to mean "average."

*few

We can't assume that this word has definite limits. One man's few is another man's several.

*get

Like several other common verbs—give, go, have, make, put, and take—"get" has extremely wide usage in slang expressions. It has nearly 11 full columns of references in the index of *The American Thesaurus of Slang* (27). The possibility of double meanings should not be overlooked when using this word.

Which salesman should get the business?
This question looks straightforward unless you realize that to "get the business" means to be "rubbed out" or killed.

*give

This word has 10 columns of references in *The American Thesaurus of Slang.*

*go

"Go" is given more space in the index of *The American Thesaurus of Slang* than any other word—a total of about 12½ columns.

When did you last go to town?
If the respondent takes this literally, it is a good question, but the "go to town" phrase has more than a dozen different slang meanings, including a couple that might get your face slapped.

*government

Here is another one of those concept words! It is sometimes used as a definite word meaning the federal government, sometimes as an inclusive term for federal, state, and local government, sometimes as an abstract idea, and sometimes as the party in power as distinct from the opposition party. The trouble is that the respondent does not always know which "government" is meant. One person may have a different idea from another.

Should the government own the electric light companies?
Which government—the federal government as in the case of TVA, or the city government as in the case of some municipal light plants, or both, or yet some other idea of government? It is best to specify if we want all respondents to answer with the same government in mind.

*have

The importance of our being aware of slang usages is well illustrated by this word which has nearly 12 columns of references in the index of *The American Thesaurus of Slang*. The following question, asked of racegoers after the Daily Double had not been offered at New York tracks for a few years, came in for some ridicule from a sportswriter:

Would you like to have the Daily Double at New York race tracks, or would you rather not have the Daily Double here?

The newspaperman wrote that in race track parlance "having the Daily Double" means having the winning ticket and that, of course, most people want to "have" the Daily Double. The fact that this particular interpretation was not detected by any of the interviewers in their more than 1,200 interviews might not be a convincing answer to the readers of the sports column.

*hear
*heard

Sometimes these words are used in a very general sense (*Have you ever heard of . . . ?*) to include learning about not only through hearing but also through reading, seeing, etc. Unfortunately, however, some respondents apparently take such words literally. They don't say that they've heard when they've only seen, for instance. In one study, mentioned earlier, only half as many people said that they had "heard or read" anything about patents as reported having attended a patents exposition. Evidently, they considered whatever they learned from attendance as separate from hearing or reading.

*it
*its

These words necessarily refer to some antecedent. You may recall the discussion of the antecedent problem in Chapter 7, where I suggested repeating the full antecedent except where it is unmistakably clear.

*just

Here is another word which has conflicting meanings. "Just as much," for example, may mean "only" as much or "fully" as much.

*knew
*know

Knowing varies greatly in degree, from mere recognition to full information.

> "Do you know about Jack?"
> "No. What about Jack?"

From this snatch of conversation it is apparent that both parties "know" Jack even though one doesn't know the latest about him. Some respondents may hesitate to say they know something when they don't know it for sure. A person may know a tune without knowing the words.

*law

This is a very powerful word to use in a question, particularly where by its use we invoke the status quo. Opposition to a proposed law usually falls off when the law is enacted. To think of changing a law is anathema to many people. Attitudes on the issue itself may be obscured by the sanctity of the law. Consequently we should always carefully consider whether to mention the law or to study the issue on its own merits.

*less

This word is usually used as an alternative to "more," where it may cause a minor problem. The phrase "more or less" has a special meaning all its own in which some respondents do not see an alternative. Thus, they may simply answer "yes, more or less" to a question like:

Compared with a year ago, are you more or less happy in your job?

The easy solution to this problem is to break up the "more or less" expression by introducing an extra word or so or to reverse the two:

Compared with a year ago, are you more happy or less happy in your job?

Compared with a year ago, are you less or more happy in your job?

*like

This word is on the problem list only because it is sometimes used to introduce an example. The problem with bringing an example into a question is that the respondent's attention may be directed toward the particular example and away from the general issue which it is meant only to illustrate. The use of examples may sometimes be necessary, but the possible hazard should always be kept in mind. The choice of an example can affect the answers to the question—in fact, it may materially change the question, as in these two examples:

Do you think that leafy vegetables like spinach should be in the daily diet?

Do you think that leafy vegetables like lettuce should be in the daily diet?

*make

Here is another component of many slang expressions, having about 7 columns of references in *The American Thesaurus of Slang*.

*might

Remember not to think of this as synonymous with "could" or "should."

*more

This word has more or less been discussed under the word "less." It is a problem for another reason also: When "more" is used in the comparative sense, it is usually advisable to indicate the basis for comparison—more than what?

Are you finding question wording more complicated?
    ... than you expected?
    ... than it was before you began this book?
    ... than selecting a sample?
    ... than the pickle business?

Sometimes, even when you might think the comparison had been completed, it is still open to misinterpretation—

Are you saving more than you did last year?
"Yes, I saved $100 last year and I'll save $200 this year."
"Yes, I saved $125 last year and I'll save $50 this year, bringing my bank account up to $175."

*most

This word can introduce tricky double thoughts like the quibbles brought up by this question:

Where would you be doing the most useful work?
Which is meant—the most work that is useful or work that is the most useful?

*much

"Much" is an indefinite word. The "how much" type of question leads to unnecessarily wide variations in response—answers in terms of dollars, doughnuts, per cents, fractions, and other measures.

*near

"Near" is a very indefinite word. How near is "near New York City," for example?

*never

This dead giveaway word reminds me of the well-bred Captain of the *Pinafore*, who had to admit that "never" was too all-embracing a term for him:

Captain:	I never use a big, big D—
Crew:	What, never?
Captain:	No, never!
Crew:	What, *never*?
Captain:	Hardly ever!

*nobody

This is yet another dead giveaway word. Nobody can use "nobody" with impunity.

*none

This also may be a dead giveaway word.

*nothing

"Nothing" is a dead giveaway in some applications.

*now

For a word that appears reasonably clear, "now" can be almost too definite in the sense of "right this minute," leading to situations like this:

> *What kind of work are you doing now?*
> "I'm answering fool questions."

*only

Sometimes this is a dead giveaway, too. In other cases, it may be prejudicial. Thus, "only a few" has a slightly different meaning than "a few."

*or

In questions this word usually introduces an alternative. Consequently it may sometimes be taken in that sense when not intended. A simple "yes" or "no" was all that was wanted for this question, but—

Is the telephone in your name or the name of someone else in your family?

*own

This definite-sounding word is not always so definite. Some home owners think that they will not own their homes until they pay off the mortgage. Some stockholders have no feeling of owning part of their company. Some people say that they have their own phone.

*people

Cantril and Fried point out that the meaning of this word may be vastly different to various respondents (23). For example, it may mean people everywhere and in all walks of life or one particular class or group of people. Answers to a question like this will vary from one part of the country to another and from one social group to another, because of narrow interpretation of "people."

Which do people eat most often—hominy grits or scrapple?

*poor

In some cases, it is possible for the rich-poor idea to get mixed in with the good-poor idea.

*possible

An alternative which uses "possible" in the ultimate sense ("as much as possible") is a dead giveaway.

*public

The natural tendency in our work to introduce our questionnaire as a "public opinion" survey may be misguided. Actually, we usually want expressions of private opinion, not the opinion one reserves for the public. Similarly, a private company is sometimes thought of as a one-owner company as distinct from "public" ownership, which may mean that ownership of shares of stock is open to the public.

*put

"Put" is another slang word, having 10 columns of references in the index of *The American Thesaurus of Slang*.

*quite

This word is quite frequently misused. "Quite a little," for example, has no sensible meaning. If in a question the word "entirely" can be substituted for "quite" without changing the meaning, then "quite" is being properly used. However, in such proper use, "quite" may become a dead giveaway word.

*read

Like "hear" and "heard" this word is sometimes used in a general sense (*Have you read about . . . ?*). Remember that "heard or read" may not include attending as far as some people are concerned.

*saw

*see

*seen

These words are sometimes used in the sense of visiting professionally but they may be interpreted literally.

> *When did you see your dentist last?*
> "Yesterday, on the golf course."

They may be subject also to some of the same problems as are "hear" and "read."

*service

Here is another indefinite word. Try, for example, to put down exactly what you mean when you speak of the "service" of the electric light company.

*several

See "few."

*should

This is one of the three little words which we showed

should not, could not, might not be used as though synonymous.

*sign

I may be dragging this problem in by the heels, but think twice before asking respondents to sign a questionnaire! Too many sharp operators are around, misrepresenting themselves as "making a survey" in order to get signatures on the dotted line. To combat this, the National Better Business Bureau, Inc., has prepared a memo to the public which says that the legitimate survey interviewer will "never ask you to sign an agreement to buy anything."

*sometimes

"Sometimes" has occasionally been inadvertently used in place of "some" with this resulting difficulty:

Sometimes people say that radio programs are getting worse all the time. Do you think they are getting better or worse?

"Well, sometimes I think they are getting worse, sometimes better."

*such

Beware of this word because it is often used to introduce examples. When we discussed "like" we pointed out that the particular example may supplant the general issue in the minds of respondents. These two questions, although meant to measure attitudes on one and the same issue, would probably bring forth different answers:

Do you approve or disapprove of women wearing slacks in public, such as while shopping?

Do you approve or disapprove of women wearing slacks in public, such as while bowling?

*supper

"Supper" may mean a substantial evening meal or a late-night snack.

*sure

This can be another dead giveaway word.

*take

Take it easy with this slang component. It has 9 columns of references in the index of *The American Thesaurus of Slang*.

*that
*these
*this
*those

These are antecedent words. Let's not use them except when we are reasonably sure that their antecedents are clear.

*the

Alfred W. Hubbard recently pointed out that the definite article "the" in a question may strongly imply the existence of the item under discussion.

Did you see the demonstration of the Foley Food Chopper in the housewares department?

In this case, the first "the" tips off the respondent that there was a demonstration of the Foley Food Chopper. She therefore may tend to answer affirmatively, although she may have paid too little attention to the demonstration even to notice the name of the gadget (51).

*today

This may be interpreted too literally, just as "now" may be.

Are farmers getting a fair price for milk today?
"Do you mean right today? You know the price dropped this morning."

*too

When used in an extreme statement, "too" may become

a dead giveaway word. Also, it may be misleading in certain idiomatic uses.

Would you say that your fellow workers are turning out enough work or that they aren't turning out too much work? In fact, the coupling of "too" with some other words can lead to a strange form of ambiguity. "You can't try too hard," has two distinct meanings—one inspirational, the other defeatist.

*town

This is a somewhat indefinite word, but in some places it has a definite meaning which is at odds with the meaning elsewhere. In Connecticut, for example, "town" is used to mean what "township" means elsewhere. In other cases, it may be used as a synonym for city—even for a very large city.

*trip

This word needs to be qualified—"one-way trip" or "round-trip," for example. A bus trip may be followed by a train trip or the combination may be thought of as a single bus-train trip.

*where

The frames of reference in answers to a "where" question may vary greatly.

> *Where did you read that?*
> "In the New York Times. "
> "At home in front of the fire."
> "In an advertisement."

Despite this seemingly wide variety of answers, some respondents could probably have stated them all: "In an ad in the New York Times while I was at home sitting in front of the fire."

*who

This is a word which can be interpreted either specifically or generally.

Who is to blame?

This question chiefly conjures up the idea of a single person, although that may not be the question's intention. A group of people, or an organization, or circumstances, or any number of people, things, or conditions might be blamed. To the extent that this wording does direct attention toward a single scapegoat, the answers might have a false specificity which a less directive question would not produce.

*you

Thoughts about "you" came ahead of everything else in this chapter.

11. Isn't that loaded?

AN ADMISSION OF GUILT, WITH EXTENUATING PARTICULARS

WHEN we speak of a question's being "loaded" or "leading," we imply that it may lead some respondents to give different answers than they would give to another wording of what was intended to be the same issue. Having read the preceding chapters, you may already have been impressed with the difficulties in producing a question that is not loaded. It may be loaded on one side, it may be loaded on the other side, or it may be loaded about evenly. In any case, you can be practically sure that it is loaded. And no one can say once and for all when it is loaded just right.

Some people raise their eyebrows at the thought of a "weighted" sample, not realizing that every sample is weighted. The sample may be weighted disproportionately or every unit may have the same weight, but in any case the sample is weighted. Similarly, every question is loaded. There is this distinction, however—we seldom have the same conviction about the proper loading of questions that we have about the proper weighting of samples. Some researchers have so little conviction about the proper loading of a question that they take whichever version happens to come out nearest the average of all versions tried in the pretest, and accept it as having the least amount of loading.

The title of this chapter is itself a loaded question, loaded heavily on one side, begging as it does for an admission. It would perhaps be more evenly loaded if it read, "Is that loaded?" or, "Is that loaded or not?" No matter how this query is worded, though, and no matter to which of our questions it may refer, the safe and honest answer is in the affirmative. "Yes, why certainly it's loaded."

Why bring that up?

The very act of bringing up some questions is a form of loading. The poet asks,

And what is so rare as a day in June?

Probably we readers have never thought before in terms of the rarity of June days. After all, they actually occur about 6 per cent more often than February days do. Yet we let the poet get away with his presumptuous question and probably nod our agreement as we read on.

Do you feel all right?

Have you left anything?

Each of these two questions brings up an issue about which the respondent may not have been thinking, but if he is at all suggestible his feelings and reactions may be noticeably affected by being asked these questions. It is possible to induce all the symptoms of illness in some people just by asking them a few questions about how they feel. This is certainly a form of loading, and it probably carries over into more questions than we realize.

Leo Crespi found that many questions have an educational (or propagandistic) force. Respondents tend to answer some questions differently when asked a second time because the first interview contributed to their knowledge or their attitudes (40).

What they would think

We should keep in mind that an opinion survey does not necessarily report what the public *is* thinking. More often it reports what the public *would* think if asked the questions. The sample of respondents becomes unrepresentative as soon as we begin eliciting opinions on questions which they and the rest of the public have not been considering. The mere act of introducing such issues is a form of loading if you choose to look at it that way.

Questions about who will win the World Series are legitimate for baseball fans, but they are loaded questions to some of the rest of us. If you ask me for my prediction in the middle of the season, I'll probably give you a definite answer even though I foolishly name a team which happens then to be in the second division. I don't know the standings, but since baseball is the great American sport, I feel that I have to give an opinion or else be counted as worse than a fool. I may not have thought at all about who will win the Series, but I get recorded perhaps as a respondent who *thinks* the Indians will win.

This kind of "public opinion" is being recorded all the time. Awareness and intensity questions help to correct for such overcounts of what the public is thinking. Even so, if we wanted to be perfectly precise about it, we probably should always report our findings as representing what the public *would* think *if* the questions were raised.

Only when the questions we ask refer to "hot" or live issues, which are being discussed by all types of people or which noticeably affect everyone, as rationing did during the war, will the answers closely approach what the people are thinking. In such cases the questions are not greatly loaded in the sense we have just been discussing.

Conviction vs. conjecture

As a matter of fact, it is usually safer to ask questions on issues where the public is stirred up than on those where it is apathetic. Where people have strong convictions, the wording of the question should not greatly change the stand they take. The question can be loaded heavily on one side or heavily on the other side, but if people feel strongly their replies should come out about the same.

It is on issues where opinion is not crystallized that answers can be swayed from one side to the other by changes in the statement of the issue. Likewise, it is on those knowledge questions where people are ignorant that their various predispositions have to be taken into account in the phrasing in order to expose the true extent of their ignorance.

Of course, there are only very few matters on which everyone can be counted upon to have strong convictions, and some people are less sure of their opinions than others are. The effect of loading is, then, just a matter of degree. Probably there is always some effect, however slight. The problem is to reduce this effect as much as we can by minimizing or equalizing the loading.

Loaded examples

Before we proceed any farther, let's take a quick look at some questions which are heavily loaded on one side. These give some idea of the extreme form of loading about which everyone including the perpetrators should have serious misgivings. This wartime questionnaire was inspired by Bill S. 1913 to create a Small Business Corporation with a billion dollars capital to succeed the much smaller Smaller War Plants Corporation. It was sent to "trade and industry associations, chambers of commerce, and other small business organizations and to individual businessmen in 48 states." It came to me as an example of the "usefulness" of opinion surveys. Here are some of the questions:

Does small business advocate the creation of another tax spending bureau for any purpose other than to aid the war effort?

"No"—96%

Does small business need a government wet nurse in all its daily activities?

"No"—97%

Would it be healthy for small business, or for the national economy, to have government loans available to all those who wish to engage in business, or enlarge their business, with the implied taxpayers' loss in case of their failure?

"No"—95%

Should not the sponsorship for the representation of, and the source of information for and about small business be embodied in a permanent, existing agency like the Department of Commerce?

"Yes"—84%

Should not such authority for small business be the subject of a separate bill for permanency?

"Yes"—80%

Should any government agency have the use of every other agency's facilities, employees or service? (It would seem that appropriations and control by Congress would be meaningless under such arrangement.) See Title 2, Sec. 2, Par. 6. (Also be sure to read the authority of the Chairman —Par. 4.)

"No"—65%

Does Title IX (1) "Provided"—grant wider discretionary powers than a good administrator would want, or a poor administrator should have?

"Yes"—69%

I leave it to the reader to guess whether the people who drafted these questions were themselves for or against the proposed bill. Also, if you wish you may attempt to assess how much the answers may have been affected by the wording of the questions. If you go so far as to wonder about the representativeness or size of the sample, no information was provided on that score.

Arthur Kornhauser raised a storm in polling circles a few years ago by a critical study of question bias which is best described in its own title, "Are Public Opinion Polls Fair to Organized Labor?" (41). The feeling of those he criticized is well summed up in the title of their rejoinder, "Is Dr. Kornhauser Fair to Organized Pollers?" (42).

In any case, it is questions of influence like these which people usually have in mind when they think about loading.

In the bulk of this chapter it is such one-sided loading we shall be talking about.

Loading for good

We should not arbitrarily condemn all one-sided loading. It is sometimes entirely legitimate to load a question heavily on one side. You can't very well evaluate sales appeals, Red Cross campaign arguments, blood bank requests, or other forms of propaganda without presenting the ideas in effective form. You can't test "a tested sentence that sells" without trying it with all of its "sell." The best means of testing the probable value of a direct mail sales campaign is to try it out on a small scale to see what returns you get— in other words, to put as much "sell" in the research approach as would be used in the campaign itself.

The loading of questions for experimental purposes may also be laudable. Word the question this way with one group of respondents and that way with a matching group. Then observe the difference in results. This split-ballot technique is the means by which we have first come to discern some forms of loading and to realize their effects.

When one-sided loading is done for ethical reasons and with eyes wide open, no one should quarrel with it. But if the same thing is done in order to present a distorted view of public opinion or the view which the questioner thinks is the "right" view, then it becomes evasion of the truth, or the direct opposite of research. If one-sided loading occurs by accident, as is most often the case, then it is simply unfortunate. The main purpose of this chapter is to explain the various forms which one-sided loading may take so that the accidental occurrences may be held to a minimum.

Backtracking

Much of the discussion in earlier chapters, although not presented as such, actually revolved around problems of loading. As the various types of questions were scrutinized and as different words were evaluated, we frequently were talking about one-sided loading and how to minimize it.

You might find it interesting to reconsider the earlier discussions in this book in terms of the bearing they may have on loaded questions. Implied alternatives, pre-coding, card lists of numbers, and dead giveaway words, to name only a few, might just as well have been discussed as forms of loading.

I preferred, however, to look upon those problems as simple mechanics rather than as examples of loading. The kinds of loading that will be described here are perhaps more spectacular or more intentional, or both, than those common garden varieties.

Status quo

"One truth is clear—Whatever is, is right."

One of the few forms of loading already touched upon (under "*law" in Chapter 10) which does perhaps deserve additional comment is the invoking of the status quo. Proposals for changing laws are unpopular, but the changes gain sudden increases in favorable opinion as soon as they are enacted. Workers on piece rates tend to prefer piece rates, while workers on hourly rates tend to prefer hourly rates. Inertia is as much a mental factor as it is a physical one.

Questions which emphasize the status quo take advantage of this strong predisposition to accept things as they are. Such questions must be considered heavily loaded. They may start with a preamble:

As you know . . .

According to the law . . .

or they may contain the idea in a phrase:

. . . as it is now . . .

. . . or should it be changed . . .

These phrases all call attention to the existing situation and almost certainly lead to higher approval than the idea would receive without this advantage.

It can always be argued that pointing to the status quo is entirely justified by the facts. The counter argument is that this does not produce an evaluation of the issue on its own merits but rather as a fait accompli, which is an entirely different matter.

There are three ways for us to dispose of these arguments. First, if practically everybody already is aware of the existing facts, then it is a matter of unimportance whether or not these facts are stated in the question. Second, if people are not so likely to know the facts, then the questioner must decide on which basis to appraise the issue—on its own merits or in the light of existing facts—so that his later interpretation of the results takes this earlier decision into account. Finally, we can always take advantage of the split-ballot technique and ask the question both ways.

Prestige

One of the most commonly recognized forms of loading is that which appeals to the very human desire for prestige. Most of us like to impress other people with our wisdom, fairness, experience, knowledge, honors, or material possessions. We may mention them casually or drag them into a conversation by the horns; and if someone shows enough interest to ask us questions, we feel especially free to make our claims for respect. We naturally want to impress our friends, but since they already know us so well, we are more likely to do our strutting before mere acquaintances or practical strangers.

The average interview is a made-to-order opportunity to indulge in this entirely natural showing off, and respondents are quick to accept the opportunity. Even though their names are not recorded, they still try to put up a good front. Or perhaps we should recognize that partly because their names will not be taken, respondents (like smoking car conversationalists) feel they can afford to be expansive—no one is likely to try to verify what they say. In any case, many evidences of prestige influences may be observed in surveys.

Respondents build up their occupational titles beyond their actual importance. Self-administered employee questionnaires often produce more "foremen" and "supervisors" than the actual payroll shows. Other members of the wage earner's family may have even more false pride than he has about his job. I recall an actual case of a man reported by his wife as a "bank director." On a later interview with him it turned out that, sure enough, his job was to "direct" the bank customers to the proper officer or window.

Educations are often similarly up-graded. False claims are frequently made of automobile ownership. Some women understate their ages. Lower income people are reputed to claim higher earnings than they actually make. Upper income people, however, are thought to discount their incomes in interviews, whether out of the prestigeful desire not to be considered boastful or to avoid disclosure for other reasons. People do not hesitate to claim readership of socially accepted newspapers, magazines, and books, but readers may deny looking at the more lurid and sensational publications. Radio listeners claim to prefer discussion programs to comedy, mystery, and musical programs, despite the actual listenership ratings to the contrary. Much the same tendencies are noted in the reporting of brands of shirts and beer, shoes and ships and sealing wax. The "blue chip" brands are overstated and the "dogs" are understated. Investigators in Denver found that large numbers of respondents, sometimes more than 10 per cent, gave exaggerated answers to questions which involved their prestige. This exaggeration appeared even on such verifiable items as possession of library cards and Community Chest contributions. (43)

More prestige

Sizeable fractions of non-voters bluff about having participated in the last election. False assertions are made by voters and non-voters alike about having supported the candidate who won. This causes a phenomenon which election pollsters call the "past preference build-up," according to which yesterday's winning candidate is credited in a survey today with a vote several percentage points higher than was actually recorded in the election.

The Kinsey report makes abundantly clear that socially tabooed sexual practices are more difficult for the interviewer to uncover than the more "normal" types of sexual activity (44). It seems evident that other less obvious taboos may operate elsewhere, such as against acknowledging paying attention to advertising. People hesitate to say that they ever read advertisements, let alone that they learn anything from them, or act upon them.

In their desire to appear well-informed, some people affect to have more knowledge than they actually possess. Hence the high proportions who are willing to give opinions on the administration of a fictitious Metallic Metals Act. In their role as judges, where some questions place them, respondents endeavor to be extremely fair. They lean over backwards not to express any unwarranted criticism.

Probably the strongest and most common prestige influence in opinion surveys is the feeling of respondents that they should have opinions. David Riesman and Nathan Glazer have discussed this in detail (45). They say that most polls assume that people will have—and subtly, therefore, that they should have—opinions on the "issues of the day" or "news of the week." No matter what the subject may be, it almost never happens on an opinion question that as many as half of the respondents admit having no opinion. "No opinion" percentages below 10 per cent are very common. Some research organizations as a matter of policy carefully instruct their interviewers how to avoid high "no opinion" replies. Other researchers have noticed that experienced interviewers, who make respondents understand that having an opinion on every question is not necessary, bring in much higher proportions of "no opinion" than the neophyte interviewer who feels that recording a "no opinion" makes the interview worthless.

Of course, there are ways of assessing the strength and validity of expressed opinions. The quintamensional plan developed by George Gallup is an approach to this problem. But there is no evident way of accomplishing all these things in a single question.

Pride pricking

The variety of examples already quoted here gives some inkling of the ever-present problem of prestige. A most straightforward factual question like *Do you own a car?* can be loaded with prestige. We must first recognize the possible existence of a prestige element and then attempt to eliminate it or counteract it. When it comes to automobile ownership, we can at least reduce the prestige element by making the question somewhat more casual and by giving the respondent a way of saving his pride. One wording that at least gives more reasonable results is:

Do you happen to own a car at present?

A somewhat similar situation is encountered when we ask people about their future intentions to buy. It brings up the old situation of wanting to bite off more than they can chew. To combat their overstatements, this double-question approach has been used with some success:

(A) *Do you plan to buy a television set in the next six months?*

(B) *Are you almost sure to buy one in the next month?*

This gives the wishful thinker the opportunity to impress

us with the idea that he will own a television set before too long, but lets him ease away from a commitment for the immediate situation, which is the situation we are interested in anyway.

We may go so far as to over-balance one prestige element with another. For example, we can start with an intensity question like this:

Do you feel reasonably sure about that or are you likely to change your mind?

In this wording, prestige acts in favor of being reasonably sure (sweet reasonableness!) and against admitting the frailty of changing one's mind. Now for a turnabout:

Do you feel sure about that or do you have an open mind?

Here prestige works for the widely approved quality of open-mindedness, while the dead giveaway use of feeling "sure" augments the tendency. Perhaps this next wording, still with some prestige, comes closer to an even balance.

Do you feel pretty sure about that or would you want to know more about it before making up your mind?

An attempt to measure intensity is a relative matter in any case, so that it may not matter much which one of the three questions is used. The value of these particular examples lies mostly in the demonstration of how easy it sometimes is to vary the prestige element.

Matter of fact

Some of the prestige in the reporting of occupations can be avoided by asking for exact job titles or for a description of duties involved. Sometimes the education question is preceded by others, asking for the name of the last school attended or the age at leaving school. Detailed questioning on various sources of income and even on expenditures helps to achieve a better total estimate of income, as in the 1936 Study of Consumer Income (46). One researcher interested in newspaper reading, upon finding that readership of tabloids was greatly understated when the question was approached directly, improved his results by asking first about favorite comic strips (even though some prestige acts against admitting any interest in the comics). During the heyday of *Gone With the Wind*, George Gallup found that an excessive proportion of respondents were claiming to have read the book. He reduced this prestige element by changing his question to, *Do you intend to read "Gone With the Wind"*? (6).

It may be hoped that sooner or later the election pollsters will find ways of eliminating or correcting the past preference build-up and other prestige elements surrounding studies of voting behavior. The Kinsey report goes to great lengths to explain the various precautions used by the interviewers to obtain full reporting of sexual activity and to show the methods of statistical verification which were used.

The prestige influence often operates in very subtle fashion and its effects are sometimes unexpected. The means of combatting it are varied and necessarily subtle themselves, so that no one or two methods can be prescribed as sure cures. The examples given here of making it easier to admit the truth, of introducing a counteracting form of prestige, of asking detailed questions, of approaching the issue through indirection, etc., may be helpful as illustrations of the devices used.

Stereotypes

One of the most spectacular forms of loading and one which has been discussed rather frequently is the influence of stereotypes, the tendency to vote for motherhood and against sin. The name of an organization, or a political party, or an individual sometimes becomes heavily charged with emotional reactions. If this name is interjected into a question, some people may react to the name instead of to the issue. It is like waving the red flag in front of the bull, for example, to introduce an issue with a statement explaining how Communists feel about it. Many respondents will vote against whichever side the Communists are said to espouse.

Selden Menefee presented a series of sixteen statements on social issues to 742 individuals and asked them to respond "Yes" or "No" to each of them. At a later date, these same questions were asked again, but each one was identified as being typical of fascism, patriotism, communism, etc. It was found that opposition to fascism brought negative changes up to 70 per cent, and opposition to communism caused more than 60 per cent of some groups to change their replies (47).

Some names have generally favorable associations, some have unfavorable ones, and others may have different but nonetheless intense associations for various groups of people. Among the personal names which could be demonstrated to have an effect on people's judgment of an issue would be such ones as Winston Churchill, Dwight Eisenhower, Henry Ford, Adolf Hitler, John L. Lewis, Douglas MacArthur, George Marshall, and Franklin D. Roosevelt. The issue itself may be overshadowed by any one of these names in a question like this:

Mr. Big says such and such. Do you agree or disagree?

It is not only proper names that act as stereotypes. Descriptive terms like "business executives" or "union leaders" may have considerable force in a question. And sometimes the different names of a particular idea will operate as different stereotypes. "Corporation" has unfavorable connotations. "Business managed" is a good symbol. "Private company" means a one-owner company to some people. "Business firm" and "business concern" evoke somewhat different impressions. "Business company" seems to be reasonably neutral and generally understood.

Issues as well as names may become stereotypes. For example, it may be one and the same thing for the state to "issue bonds" and for the state to "go into debt." Both are honest statements, but the first may be thought of as a euphemism for the second. "Going into debt" is a strong negative stereotype. Which way should the question be phrased? Someone with stronger convictions will have to answer that. How about a split ballot?

Here is a particularly blatant example of loading through the introduction of a stereotype:

Which would you say is contributing most to the war effort—government, industry, or labor union leaders?

Neither of the first two alternatives is very clear. Both of them, government and industry, are "blab" words. But how completely unfair it is to stack up those two general ideological terms against the stereotype of "labor union leaders"! Why single out a relative few individuals for comparison with all of government and industry? Far more equitable would be a question in which the alternatives were "government, industry, or labor."

Sterile opinion?

There cannot be a hard and fast rule against stereotypes, however. The realities of the situation may link the issue and the stereotype so closely together that they have to be treated as one. It might be possible to word a perfectly sterile question on such an interconnected issue in order to get a measure of sterile opinion—that is, if anyone wanted to think of public opinion as sterile. Still, one can't very reasonably separate the name out of such things as the Damon Runyon Cancer Fund, the Edison Electric Institute, or the Kentucky Derby. The name itself is a considerable part of the idea. Even when we speak of the Derby the full name is clearly implied, and it is certainly something more than just another horse race!

Some names are so ingeniously contrived in their use of stereotypes that they virtually defeat the researcher who would like to learn the public's appraisal of the idea they represent. "Facts" are such a strong stereotype, for example, that you can hardly think of asking the public what it thinks of a "Fact Finding Board"! Here the name is probably more important in gaining public acceptance than the actual idea it represents. What I am saying is that where public opinion is largely based on the name it is unrealistic to disassociate the issue from that name.

In such cases, try it both ways! The split-ballot technique will help you to understand the structure of opinion—how much approval or disapproval is based on the issue, how much on the name?

Dead giveaways

At the risk of seeming repetitious, it is probably worthwhile to amplify further on the form of loading that makes use of the dead giveaway. You have seen so many mentions of dead giveaway words in the last chapter that you may feel that the subject has been covered more than thoroughly. Nevertheless, the dead giveaway recurs in actual practice so often that another example or two of a slightly different sort may not be wasted.

Sometimes the dead giveaway consists of a phrase instead of a single word. But it may nonetheless be a serious problem. Here is one such question which college teachers answered somewhat differently from the general public:

Would you say it's better to regulate business pretty closely, or would you say the less regulation of business the better?

	GENERAL PUBLIC	COLLEGE TEACHERS
Pretty closely	35%	30%
Less the better	52	33
No choice	13	37

If we care to be literal about it, and perhaps some of the

teachers were this literal, "the less regulation the better" really comes down to no regulation at all. We can't tell from these answers whether there is an ideological difference between the public and the teachers or merely that teachers are more sophisticated in interpreting the question.

Are there any people in the junk business who make more money than they should?

Of course there are! Every business probably includes some people who make more money than they should.

Do you think there are people in the pickle business who would cheat you if they could?

Of course! Cheats are everywhere, except in research.

Could the mayor do a better job of running the city, or not?

Of course, he could! Only a few of us are perfect.

Examples of other dead giveaway phrases:

all they can	as well as possible
best they can	as well as able
doing his best	more the merrier

Yet another form of dead giveaway can result from being too specific.

Do you believe that industry spends five million dollars a year on opinion research?

In answering this question, it is possible that some respondents will express disbelief because they don't think the figure is *exactly* five million. Some qualification in the question would help, such as ". . . about five million dollars. . . ."

The dead giveaway is one form of loading which can be labeled with a great big DON'T. So far, I have seen no virtues claimed for it.

Means versus ends

"People frequently give answers about ends when the question deals with means to ends." This problem has been discussed at length in *The Public Opinion Quarterly* (48).

The questions used there had to do with social medicine, and the paper showed that people were so desirous of the good end of prepayment medical care that they would approve it under any guise—government medicine, insurance company plans, or doctor-sponsored plans. The mistake that could so easily be made in this situation would be to ask about only one of these means of achieving the good end and then to decide that because of its high approval it was *the* particular means the public wanted.

I prefer a more homely although far-fetched illustration of the confusion of means and ends. Suppose we should get a very high proportion of affirmative answers to this question:

Do you like Delicious apples?

The Delicious Apple Growers Association might take this result and proclaim it to the world: "Eight people in every ten like *Delicious* apples!" Perhaps, however, the respondents aren't thinking particularly of the Delicious variety but of apples generally. Just as many might if given the opportunity say that they like *Jonathan* apples, or *Winesaps*, or *Transparents*, or other varieties. Their answers are not necessarily distinguishing so far as varieties are concerned, even though somebody might wish to interpret them that way.

Thus, the loading in the means-versus-ends situation occurs as much in the interpretation of results as in the wording of the question. The principle deduced in the *Quarterly* article was this: When a question is asked about means, it is important to determine whether respondents actually testify about means or about ends.

Circumstantial loading

Sometimes outside influences at the time of asking the question or circumstances in the interview have a decided effect on the answers. In the interview itself, this sequence of questions would have a noticeable effect on answers to the second one:

Do you ever listen to Bob Hope on the radio?

What are your favorite radio programs?

It is enough to discuss the wording of individual questions here without getting into all the details of questionnaire construction, but one important principle of design, brought out by this illustration, should be mentioned. Reversing the order of asking the two questions would eliminate the inter-action—not having been reminded of Bob Hope, respondents would not have him at the top of their consciousness when asked about their favorite programs. So the important principle is: Proceed from the general to the specific.

Outside circumstances can also have a decided effect on the answers to a question. For example, in the Spring of 1947, when the price of aluminum was at an all-time low, few people gave correct answers to this question:

What about the price of aluminum—has it gone up, gone down, or stayed the same in the last year?

Gone up	47%
Stayed the same	9
Gone down	7
Don't know	37

The fact that almost half of the public said that the price of aluminum had gone up does not mean that they really thought this of aluminum specifically. Rather, they probably were judging that, since the price of almost everything was up, the price of aluminum must be up also.

This signifies that the answers to a question should be interpreted with reference to existing circumstances. Other questions on related subjects usually help to highlight these situations. In other words, the question should not be asked as an isolated issue if it actually is surrounded with important circumstances.

Known versus unknown

The situation sometimes arises where one of the alternatives presented to respondents is much better known than the other and hence is selected more often. The clearest example I think of comes at the start of a political race between a well-known public figure and a politically unknown challenger.

If the election for Governor were being held today, which candidate would you vote for—Morey Pute or Bob Scure?
If Pute has been in office for twenty years, while Scure has never been in the limelight before, the results of this question at the start of the campaign may indicate an overwhelming victory for Pute. It may be advisable to identify Scure in the question at least as well as he will be identified on the actual ballot.

Which candidate will you vote for—Mr. Pute, the Democrat, or Mr. Scure, the Republican?
This attempt at balancing the loading through bringing party affiliation into account is much more likely to approximate the actual returns than is the first version.

Personalization

Strange differences are sometimes observed between what a person says about himself and what he says about his fellows, or even what he says about his group including himself. Cantril and Rugg report, for example, that more people thought certain things should be done "even if it means more taxes" than thought these same things should be done "even if you have to pay a special tax."

For another illustration, let us refer to two questions which both have to do with hospital insurance, but one is personalized while the other is not (48). First, the personalized question:

If you could get some insurance for which you paid a certain amount each month to cover any hospital care you might

need in the future, would you rather do that or would you rather pay the hospital what it charges you each time?
Next, the impersonalized version:

Some people have a kind of insurance for which they pay a certain amount each month to cover any hospital care they or their families may have in the future. Do you think this is a good idea or a bad idea?

PERSONALIZED		IMPERSONALIZED	
Prefer insurance	66%	Good idea	92%
Rather pay each time	28	Bad idea	4
No opinion	6	No opinion	4

Thus, by changing from a personalized speak-for-yourself-John question to a general one which allows respondents to answer more altruistically or with less consideration of personal consequences, approval of prepayment hospital insurance is increased by 26 percentage points.

In employee studies, more criticism can usually be elicited in terms of "the people you work with" than in terms of "you yourself." Consequently it is sometimes argued that the indirect non-personalized question succeeds better in getting personalized evaluations than the direct personalized version does. Be that as it may, the fact is clear that different results are obtained according to the degree of personalization. Cantril and Rugg do not give a cut-and-dried rule for making a decision about which version to use: "Where one does have a choice between personalized and nonpersonalized forms, it is simply a matter of deciding which form presents the issue more realistically and which is more appropriate to the particular purposes of investigation" (17).

We might add that the choice can be avoided and better understanding of the structure of opinion can be achieved if the problem is ducked through use of the split-ballot technique. Sometimes the distinction between the personalized and impersonalized versions is so great that both variations can be asked in the same questionnaire. It is possible that even in the above case on hospitalization insurance, both questions could have been asked in a single interview.

Hypotheticals

In answer to hypothetical questions all the way from *What would you do with a million dollars?* to *What things would be most important to you in buying a refrigerator?* respondents are prone to give what might be thought of as "normal" answers. These normal answers, while they sound all right and look reasonable enough, may not tie in with the actual facts of behavior at all. A housewife who says that the size of the refrigerator is most important to her may with little regard for size look high and low to get one with a left-hand door when next she makes an actual purchase. She may say that she is loyal to her present brand of vacuum cleaner, but next day allow a salesman to talk her into buying another brand.

Respondents, like other people, are very poor at predicting the future, even their own future behavior. They make mistakes in their forecasts for themselves from one hour to the next, let alone from one week to another, or from this year to a year from now. John Dollard has given seven conditions which may affect the relationship between a respondent's answer and his actual behavior (49).

Practically every one of us has had an experience of going into a store to buy a blue suit and coming out with a brown one, or something as unpredictable. Back in the fourth chapter, when discussing the questions the housewife may answer in buying a frying pan, I was talking about a hypothetical purchase. In an actual case, she might very well answer all the questions listed there in favor of a certain frying pan, but then decide to take another if the heft and swing of it were more to her liking. If she had been asked in advance, she very likely would never have thought about flingability as an important consideration.

If hypothetical questions bring hypothetical answers, then the way to obtain factual answers is to ask factual questions. Many hypothetical questions can be recast into a factual mold. We can sometimes learn most about future purchasing behavior by asking questions about the purchase of the *present* refrigerator or of the *last* frying pan. Actual experience is often a better guide to the future than present intentions are.

It requires considerable strength of conviction for us to change a question into the past tense when our interest lies in the future. Yet, it is possible that our predictions can be improved thereby. In questions of election turnout, for example, the people who did not vote last time are probably least likely to vote the next time, no matter what protestations of good intention they may make about it.

Sometimes a hypothetical question is the only kind that can reasonably be asked. In such cases, it is important that it be interpreted hypothetically in *all* its parts, or else a strange mixture of realistic and hypothetical answers may result. The only way to describe this problem is by example.

If you had a friend who was looking for a job, which company here in town would you recommend to him?

Answers to this question may leave out a company that is generally acknowledged to be a good employer. The reason may be simply that respondents know that the company is not hiring anybody now. In other words, they see that there would actually be no use in recommending this company to a job seeker. A revised version might be:

If you had a friend who was looking for a job and jobs could be had at any company, which company here in town would you recommend to him?

Standards for comparison

Blankenship says that the questions must be phrased in psychologically concrete and specific terms (6). Among other things, he points out that a person could not be asked a direct question on the food value of milk. Such an attitude could be secured, however, by inquiring:

Which do you consider more nourishing: a glass of milk, a half pound of potatoes, two eggs, or a half pound of string beans?

People often need some such standards of comparison. An example of this is the one on symbolized numbers quoted earlier. In attempting to determine how large the national public thought a certain company was, a direct question was first asked about the number of its employees. Respondents proved hopelessly at a loss to answer this question. Next they were asked to compare it with other large companies, but since they had only vague ideas about all these companies, they were still lost for an answer. It finally ended up by giving them two handles for the idea, the names of the companies *and* the numbers of their employees. This question seemed to come closer to home for them—that is, three-fourths of the respondents did at least hazard a guess.

Which of these companies would you say it comes closest to in number of employees—General Motors with 350,000 employees, Sears, Roebuck with 70,000, National Cash Register with 12,000, or Florsheim Shoe with 3,000?

Extensive questions

Many factual questions needlessly attempt to cover too much territory and therefore become almost hypothetical themselves. *How many eggs do you fry in a year?* or *How many ice cubes do you use in a year?* Both are factual enough, but they are stated in such unfamiliar or inconvenient terms that they lead to guesses. The housewife has to think in terms of a much shorter time and multiply up to obtain the annual totals. If she thinks of it, she may make approximate adjustments for the season of the year. Like as not, her estimate won't be very good.

To save her the trouble, we can ask about her egg frying and ice cube making yesterday or last week. These estimates will, of course, be more accurate for the shorter time period, and by asking the question at various times of the year will give basic data for greatly improved annual estimates.

Detailed questions, better than extensive ones, put ideas in terms that are easy to grasp. The detailed question brings the subject down to a comprehensible basis. In the Consumer Purchases Study, for example, people were not asked directly how much in total they spent for recreation last year. Better estimates were obtained by asking separately about movie attendance by seasons split by adults and children, about plays, pageants, concerts, lectures, forums, ball games, other spectator sports, dances, circuses, and fairs. Next, figures were obtained on the amounts spent for each sport: equipment, supplies, fees, licenses, hunting, fishing, camping, trapping, hiking, riding, baseball, tennis, golf, bicycling, skating, sledding, skiing, billiards, bowling, boating, cards, chess, and other games. And this was not all; questions were also asked about radios, musical instruments, sheet music, records, cameras, photo supplies, toys, play equipment, pets, entertaining, and dues to clubs (46).

Such detailed questioning has several advantages over a single extensive question. In this case, the detail serves to define the term "recreation." Everyone understands that photo supplies are included, for example. The detailed questions serve as effective reminders. The money spent in the bowling league games might otherwise be overlooked. If the detail is complete enough, then the total is more accurate than it would be on a broad overall estimate. In addition, of course, the answers to the detailed questions are often of value in themselves. Their disadvantage, of course, is in the amount of time they require in the interview. It all comes down to a question of how accurate the replies need be.

The difference between extensive and detailed inquiries can be illustrated in opinion surveys as well as in factual studies. I have a good example at hand in a survey of one company's employees. On this free-answer question, only 28 per cent mentioned something they wanted to know about the company:

Is there anything about the company on which you would like more information?

But when asked directly about only this one feature of the company's operations, 69 per cent indicated that they were interested in learning more about it:

Would you like to know more about other departments in the company, or do you know all you want to know about the other departments?

A load off my mind

Perhaps I appear to have strayed rather far away from the subject of loaded questions toward the end of this chapter. If that seems to be the case, please allow me to take refuge in my original definition that a loaded question is one which may lead some respondents to give different answers than they would give to another wording of what was intended to be the same issue. Under this definition "loading" is the subject of the entire book anyway, just as "taking too much for granted" is.

12. How does it read?

A SHORT LESSON IN PUNCTUATION, PHONETICS, ABBREVIATIONS, ETC.

QUESTIONS which have taken into consideration all the factors already discussed may still contain certain more or less mechanical difficulties. Punctuation, emphasis, position of the alternatives, pronunciation, abbreviations, all may affect the answers to our questions. If all of our interviewers were to read each question in the same level monotone with the same sounds and at the same rate of speed, and if all respondents were to wait until hearing the entire question before formulating their answers, these items of mechanical construction would be of little consequence.

Such is not the case, however. Some interviewers speak rapidly, some slowly. Some of them use little emphasis in reading the questions, others sound like students of elocution. Most respondents politely wait out the question, but some leap to conclusions before all the alternatives are stated. In this chapter we shall discuss some of these problems and various ways of meeting them.

Why do you say that?

A popular form of the reason-why question is the one which reads, *Why do you say that?* One researcher, observing that one of his interviewers appeared to be having unusual difficulty with a questionnaire, asked her to repeat one of her interviews with him. Her interviewing progressed very smoothly until she reached this question, where her intonation placed undue emphasis on the last word:

Why do you say THAT?

The note of incredulity which this inflection brought into the interview explained the interviewer's difficulty. After correcting it, she was able to continue her work with no further problems.

Just to emphasize to yourself what misplaced emphasis can do to a simple question, you may want to try the exercise of repeating this question aloud, accenting one word and then another:

WHY do you say that?
Why DO you say that?
Why do YOU say that?
Why do you SAY that?
Why do you say THAT?

It makes a real difference, doesn't it?

Underscoring

Some words do require special emphasis and it is important to insure that the interviewers do emphasize them. The use of italics or underlining is an effective means of accomplishing this.

What companies come into your mind as makers of <u>small motor trucks</u>?

What about <u>hourly</u> rates of pay—do you think they will go up, go down, or stay about the same during the next year?

The fact that emphasis is indicated for some words in a questionnaire may help to show our interviewers that other words should not be emphasized. In addition, we should caution them not to use special inflection except where it is specifically called for.

Gun jumpers

The bane of the question worder's existence is the respondent who anticipates the question and gives an answer before the question is half out of the interviewer's mouth. After the careful work that has gone into preparation of the question, it is disheartening when people won't take the time to listen to it.

But sometimes we question worders may be responsible in part for the fact that our respondents jump the gun. We may have so stated the first part of the question that the choices seem obvious to them or so that they are willing to waive whatever special conditions they may not yet have come to. We must keep in mind that the question must hold respondent interest through the last word. We must not tip our hand too early.

Cart after horse

The surest way for us to avoid premature answers is to save the key idea until the last and then to state it as briefly as possible. Usually this key idea is provided in the alternatives, which means that they should ordinarily be placed at the end of the question.

In the following question, respondents may think they can answer as soon as they hear the word "pessimistic" or the word "outlook."

Would you say that businessmen you know are optimistic or pessimistic about the business outlook for the next year?

If the last eight qualifying words are of any importance, which they should be or else be deleted, then some respondents are going to miss them. It may seem a bit awkward, but the following rearrangement should force all respondents to listen through to the end.

Would you say that most businessmen you know, in looking at the business outlook for the next year, are optimistic or pessimistic?

A rule that applies generally is that conditional clauses should come early in the question. No one can miss this qualification for instance:

If you were enlisting, how would you like to be in the Signal Corps?

If the question were reversed, however, the response could

be different because some people might answer before the condition was stated:

How would you like to be in the Signal Corps if you were enlisting?

Here is another example from an earlier chapter:

Would you say the present price of gasoline is high, about right, or low in comparison with the prices of other things you buy?

Possibly some early answering respondents may have missed the point of comparison in this version. A version which reads just as well, but which would not be subject to this misinterpretation, is:

In comparison with the prices of other things you buy, would you say the present price of gasoline is high, about right, or low?

I should point out, however, that the argument for placing the alternatives toward the end of the question is not accepted by all researchers. Gallup and Rae, for example, state the direct opposite as one of their seven criteria for question wording: "Where the individual is being asked to choose between different alternatives, this choice of alternatives must be given as early in the question as possible" (50). I gather that they are mainly concerned with avoiding the possible confusion from a question which causes respondents to start thinking in one direction and then ends with an unexpected issue, like that old riddle about "how many were going to St. Ives?"

Perhaps one way to resolve this matter is to state that since we all want to avoid the confusing preambles and long-winded queries anyway, we should strive to shorten the distance between start and end of all our questions. If the alternatives come as early as possible and toward the end at the same time, then everyone's requirement is met.

Again, this difference of opinion gives me another chance

to suggest more experimenting with the split-ballot technique.

Comma fault

The use of punctuation marks at some points in a question may be conducive to early answers. Commas, colons, dashes, and periods indicate pauses in speech, and unfortunately even a slight pause may be taken by some respondents as marking the end of the question. Recall the one "loose" question from Chapter 8 for which the alternative stated first had the greater drawing power. Read it here slowly and carefully, as some interviewers do, and you will see how the respondent might interject his answer during either one of the indicated pauses and before hearing the second alternative:

Do you think the oil companies hold back new developments—such as ways for increasing gasoline mileage—or that they are quick to adopt new developments?

The same problem arises with the alternate version:

Do you think the oil companies are quick to adopt new developments—such as ways for increasing gasoline mileage —or that they hold back new developments?

It is only a hypothesis that the dashes may have had an effect on the answers to this question, but the logic of this possible explanation seems reasonable.

In any case it will do little harm if we set up a rule for ourselves that the part of the question which states the alternatives should not be broken up with punctuation any more than is absolutely necessary. This does not mean that essential punctuation should not be used in the question. It does mean that the "comma fault," which we heard so much about in Freshman English, may be as serious a problem in question wording as in other forms of communication. The above question might have been asked this way, with much less danger of early answers:

Some people say that the oil companies are quick to adopt new developments—such as ways for increasing gasoline mileage. Others say that the oil companies hold back new developments. Which do you think?

Of course, this version is far from ideal in other respects, but at least the punctuation is not so likely to encourage premature responses.

Pickled peppers

While we are discussing these details of construction, there are some other pitfalls which should be mentioned. Among these are pronunciation difficulties.

An earlier illustration showed the possible confusion which may result with words like "lead" and "wind." Other words like "draught" in draught beer may seem hard to pronounce, but if we are careful to use only familiar words and the simpler spellings (like "draft") we should have little of this difficulty.

Sometimes it is impossible to avoid using a word of strange pronunciation like "Taliaferro" or "Worcester." In such cases, a parenthetical statement to the interviewer may be very helpful.

Who do you think will win—Brown or Taliaferro (pronounced Tolliver)?

Have you ever been in Worcester (pronounced Wooster)?

Tongue twisters should, of course, be avoided, and certainly it isn't necessary to use wordings like this in our questions:

How many pecks of pickled peppers did Peter Piper pick?

Words like "very" and "fairly" sound very much alike, which makes them somewhat ill-suited for use as alternatives in the *very good, fairly good, or not very good* sense.

Words that sound alike also lead to confusion as in the familiar riddle about the newspaper:

What is black and white and read all over?

Sometimes, if our interviewers speak at all indistinctly, a word of somewhat similar sound may be taken for the intended word. One of my colleagues, for example, was somewhat shocked to learn that an acquaintance thought he was engaged in "opium" research.

Wherever possible, then, we should avoid the use of confusing homographs, homonyms, and alliterations, as well as words that are difficult or confusing in pronunciation.

Spelling it out

Abbreviations are out of place in a question which is meant to be read aloud. Imagine the dilemma of the interviewer who has been told to read questions *exactly* as they are written when he comes to the unpronounceable "etc."! Of course, he will have to disregard his literal instructions in order to substitute the "et cetera" or "and so forth." But which one of these is he expected to say? The questionnaire might just as well spell it out for him.

Or, take an idea like "½ doz." This may be stated as "one-half dozen," "half a dozen," "a half dozen," or "a half a dozen." Now, the choice of wordings here may seem like six of one or a half dozen of the other, but making the small decision can be momentarily perplexing to the interviewer, who may hesitate or even stumble over the translation. Again, since it is so simple to do, we might as well spell it out.

As for that preposterous back-handed method of describing large amounts of money—"$3 billion"—let's try to be straightforward about it and write it out, "three billion dollars"!

$, %, or fractions

The word "much" as used in the "how much" approach was called a problem word because it leads to such a wide variety of replies. One question that illustrates this problem very well was asked as a bottle of orange-drink was shown to respondents (52).

How much orange juice do you think it contains?

Here are some of the different kinds of answers which this indefinite question brought forth:

"One orange and a little water and sugar."

"25% orange and 75% carbonated water."

"Juice of one-half dozen oranges."

"3 ounces of orange juice."

"Full-strength."

"A quarter cup of orange juice."

"None."

"Not much."

"A small amount of orange juice."

"One-fourth orange juice."

"Very little, if any, orange juice."

"Doubt it."

"Don't know."

"Not very much."

"3 to 4 ounces of orange juice."

"Part orange juice."

"A pint." (Probably referring to the size of the bottle.)

"Most of it."

"A little water mixed with orange juice."

"About a glass and a half." (Probably referring to the total contents of the bottle, not the composition of the drink.)

Answers like these lead to tabulation nightmares and indicate also that the respondents do not know for sure what the question means. It would have been much simpler for everyone if the question had read something like this, for example:

This bottle holds sixteen ounces of a drink. How many ounces of that would you say is orange juice?

Or—

What percentage of this drink would you say is orange juice?

Answers in fractions would be more difficult to elicit without influencing the replies, because it almost always seems necessary to illustrate what is meant by the word "fractions," and then the illustrations used are likely to be the ones played back by respondents.

What part of this drink—a quarter, a half, three-quarters, or what—would you say is orange juice?

In this version, answers would almost certainly cluster on the three fractions used as examples.

Similar problems occur in other types of questions, where the "how much" term itself is not used. For example:

What part of each dollar the company takes in would you say goes for wages?

Answers to such a question will be given in percentages, cents, fractions, approximate fractions, and in vague terms such as "not very much." The question might better have read:

How many cents out of each dollar the company takes in would you say goes for wages?

Our questions might just as well make clear whether answers are wanted in terms of actual figures or relative values. Answers of "five million dollars" or of "six per cent" would be equally appropriate to this question:

What profit did the company make last year?

Yet the wording could easily have clarified whether dollar or percentage replies were wanted.

Just one more example of the need for establishing what are the desired standards of measurement:

Which State is larger—New York or Texas?

What is meant—area or population?

Yes, my darling daughter

Some questions which are in no way ambiguous themselves

may tend to produce ambiguous answers. Not that the questions are so wilfully misinterpreted as in the case of that old chestnut:

How many people work in your office?
"Oh, about half of them, I should say."
The type of ambiguous answer I mean here is the "Yes, I mean no" variety. You will no doubt remember the paradoxical reply of the doting mother in the old ditty:

> "Mother, may I go out to swim?"
> "Yes, my darling daughter:
> Hang your clothes on a hickory limb
> And don't go near the water."

At one stage of World War II, when additional manpower and womanpower were urgently needed in certain war centers, a national survey asked a question like:

Would you be willing to take a war job in some other locality?
One young girl who answered "Yes" amplified her statement in this way, "I'd be glad to take a war job in Podunk because my father drives over there everyday anyway." Her original affirmative answer thus was changed to a negative or intermediate one because she signified no real willingness to move any distance to take a war job. If the idea of a major move had been more clearly stated in the question, this ambiguous answer would have been avoided.

Trend

Finally and almost always, we should be concerned not only about how the question reads *now*, but also about how it *will* read several years from now if we should have occasion to repeat it. Wherever possible, our questions should be worded so that they can be repeated at a later date for trend comparisons. Some issues, it is true, are so tied to current events that they cannot be projected into the future. But other questions which cover almost timeless issues too often become dated because the original wording needlessly mentioned some then-current event.

Surveys during World War II, for example, had a rash of questions beginning with the words, "After the war. . . ." Not one of these questions can safely be used as a trend question now that that war is over. Today the same issues are being stated in terms of "Two or three years from now . . . ," which may destroy comparability with the earlier versions. We would have been more farsighted if we had used the present version even during wartime.

The test which we can apply to almost every question is to ask whether this will read satisfactorily five years from now and whether it would have read satisfactorily five years ago. If the answer to these hypothetical questions is "Yes," we may proceed with less fear for the future.

13. Is it possible?

A VISUAL DEMONSTRATION OF THE DEVELOPMENT OF A PASSABLE QUESTION

Now for an attempt at wording a question from the first statement of the issue to the point where it is ready for pretesting. Let us not make fools of ourselves, however. Just so that neither you nor I need feel self-conscious about the stupidities that may come to light, I suggest that we induce a third party to carry out the experiment for us. And I have a man in mind for the job, too. But I don't want to embarrass him either, so I'll conceal his identity by using only his initials, S. P.

We ought to confront him with an issue that is not too easy to put into shape for general public consumption but which is not entirely impossible for laymen to answer either. In other words, let him try one that is typical of the tough problems we question worders are up against most of the time. As good for this purpose as any issue we are likely to find is that horrible example of a general public question with which I began the second chapter.

Which do you prefer—dichotomous or open questions?

(1)

We must admit one virtue in the issue as it is stated here: it is short and to the point. It is a safe bet that our friend, S. P., won't succeed in holding it down to anything like its present eight words. What we realize and he may not understand is that one precise term used by the technician often does the work of many more common words. That's the conflict between precision and brevity on the one side and familiarity and wide usage on the other. A single word like "dichotomous" has to be replaced by several more general words to define it, or make it intelligible, for the layman.

[214]

Let's ask S. P. to take this problem step-by-step, even though he might be tempted to essay it in one big jump. If at the same time he happens to make a few false starts, it won't be the first time such mistakes have been made. Besides, he can probably learn more fundamentals through a plodding trial-and-error approach than by a brilliant or intuitive leap to the conclusion.

And don't let him start rephrasing this as a question for respondents until we are reasonably sure that all of us are in agreement about the issue ourselves. In his recent treatise on sampling Dr. Deming lists seventeen errors common to both complete counts and samples, of which the first is "failure to state the problem carefully and to decide just what statistical information is needed" (53). If we can agree about what we want to get out of this issue and can be sure that its meaning is unmistakably clear to us, then it will be time enough to let S. P. try to make it meaningful to respondents.

Is this issue at all meaningful to us? Well, it certainly ought to be. We have spent a lot of time discussing the advantages and disadvantages of the various types of questions. And even though I once tried to dismiss the issue as a bootless argument, I'm sure that other people will not soon stop discussing it. In that case, the preferences of respondents should have some bearing on the matter. At least, it would be helpful to know how they feel about it, if they are able to tell us.

The issue is not as meaningful as it might be if it were complete, however. It presents only two of the three major varieties of questions. We could conceivably leave the multiple-choice type out of consideration, but if you and S. P. have no objections, I'd like to put that third candidate on the ballot. In a sense, the multiple-choice question is the compromise candidate since it fits between the other two types, but I don't expect that many respondents will realize that it is the middle-ground alternative.

Which do you prefer—dichotomous, MULTIPLE-CHOICE, or open questions? (2)

Notice that we have now changed the question itself from a dichotomous to a multiple-choice question.

S. P. may be satisfied that the statement now is a complete and adequate expression of the issue, but let's see whether it stands up under the Who?-Why?-When?-Where?-How? appraisal. It's clear enough that the Who is the respondent. The Why doesn't apply here. The answer to the When and Where is "In a survey." Maybe we ought to make this last idea clear.

Which do you prefer IN SURVEYS—dichotomous, multiple-choice, or open questions? (3)

S. P., beginning to catch on, interjects here that we ought to explain the kind of survey. After all, some people might prefer categorical questions in census surveys and free-answer questions in opinion surveys. Perhaps he has a possible point, so:

Which do you prefer in OPINION surveys—dichotomous, multiple-choice, or open questions? (4)

That leaves only the How to be answered, and apparently the only thing that isn't stated so far is whether we mean preference as a questioner or as a respondent. That's easy enough to take care of:

Which do you prefer TO BE ASKED in opinion surveys—dichotomous, multiple-choice, or open questions? (5)

There, that does it. The issue is defined completely and precisely. All that remains to be done is to let S. P. convert it into understandable form for the man on the street. We'll have to make sure that in converting it he doesn't stray away from the issue as it is now defined. Let's remember this version, number 5, as the one his final wording has to paraphrase.

[216]

Now that we know what the issue is, we can judge whether it is meaningful to the public. I think you will agree that the concept of three types of questions is not, whether we are talking about the present wording or any other wording. The public cannot be expected to have thought about this matter before. This is not the kind of issue that provokes debate in the press or on the radio. It's practically a nonentity to everyone except public opinion pollers.

S. P. is at first inclined to argue that we have no corner on asking questions. He says that everybody does it. The experience is universal. Not only that, he says, but people are familiar with all these kinds of questions—they use them all the time. He is stopped, though, when we explain that questions just come naturally to most people, but that we make work out of ours. Other people don't give a thought to the type of question they are asking. We are the strange ones who are concerned about the characteristics of form. He finally admits that maybe people don't give much consideration to question types, but strongly affirms that he thinks they ought to.

What we have is an uncommon query about a very common thing—something like asking which variety of wood you like best in a pencil. You will remember that I first used this issue on question types to illustrate the problem of taking things for granted. We are going to have to be very careful about that in this case. A colorless subject that people have never thought about presents a more difficult wording problem than an issue on which we know that respondents have strong feelings. Even when respondents finally understand what we are driving at, I'm afraid that the idea will at best be vaguely unfamiliar to them. Our biggest problem will be to make this issue come alive for them.

S. P. has an inspiration: "Why not ask it this way?", he suggests, "Put it at the end of a questionnaire and explain that we are referring to surveys like the one they have just been interviewed on. Then we'll be sure that respondents have just had experience with each of the three types."

Now, that sounds like a good idea! It's the kind of approach that can change an ethereal abstraction into meat and potatoes that people can sink their teeth into. If we can get respondents to realize that we are talking about something no farther away than the questions they just answered, we will have some chance of making the issue meaningful to them.

Which do you prefer to be asked in opinion surveys LIKE THIS—dichotomous, multiple-choice, or open questions?
(6)

"Opinion" is redundant when we are speaking of "surveys like this," so let's suggest to S. P. that he drop it.

Which do you prefer to be asked in surveys like this— dichotomous, multiple-choice, or open questions? (7)

That still sounds more hypothetical than it need be. To carry S. P.'s idea a little farther, let's suggest that he put it in the past tense and stick to this particular survey.

Which DID you prefer to be asked in THIS SURVEY— dichotomous, multiple-choice, or open questions? (8)

Now the "to be asked" is practically unnecessary, since the respondent is definitely on the receiving end when we speak of "this survey":

Which did you prefer in this survey—dichotomous, multiple-choice, or open questions? (9)

S. P. thinks that he would like to try another slightly different angle and get away from the stilted "prefer" at the same time.

Which TYPE OF QUESTION DID YOU LIKE BEST in this survey—dichotomous, multiple-choice, or open? (10)

Since we end up the question with the three *types* of questions, the "type of" may not be needed. Furthermore, the distinction between "questions" and "type of question" looks like a distinction without a difference as far as most people will notice.

Which QUESTIONS did you like best in this survey— dichotomous, multiple-choice, or open? (11)

S. P. is really beginning to identify himself with the whole idea. Now he would like to substitute for "in this survey."

Which OF MY questions did you like best—dichotomous, multiple-choice, or open? (12)

This makes me wonder whether the past tense doesn't enable us to get along without either phrase, thus:

Which questions did you like best—dichotomous, multiple-choice, or open? (13)

We've gone a long way around to get the preamble into this shape and it may still present some problems. Perhaps the antecedent isn't clear, so that we will have to reinstate the "in this survey" phrase. Maybe the "type of question" distinction would make a difference. Those are two problems which we can earmark for the pretest. S. P. wants to get on with the alternatives, so let's see what he can do with "dichotomous":

. . . TWO-WAY . . . (14)

Would you want to bet that our unimaginative respondent will know what is meant by a "two-way question"? It is a translation of "dichotomous" all right, but it still would require explanation. The meaning of the phrase in this context is very specialized, even if it is logical. Our respondent could figure it out eventually, but let's ask S. P. to try again.

. . . two-way QUESTIONS LIKE YES-NO . . . (15)

Oh, oh! He had better back away from the example idea fast. In the first place, some respondents will think strictly of the Yes-No example rather than the general two-way type it is supposed to illustrate. In the second place, an example for one of the three types demands an example for each of the others, which would be just too much and too difficult.

What if he spells out the two-way idea, like this:

*. . . THOSE THAT GAVE YOU ONLY ONE
CHOICE . . .* (16)

Technically, that's right for a two-way question. It affords *one* choice—the one choice of this or that. Still, there would be those who would not understand it clearly unless we called it "two choices." Consequently, because it is important to get the correct idea over and because there is a question of whether it should read one choice or two, let's ask S. P. to try again without that unfortunate word.

*. . . those that gave you only TWO ANSWERS TO
CHOOSE BETWEEN . . .* (17)

Do you suppose that S. P. is prejudiced against the two-way question? In both his last two trys he has used "only" in a way that might be taken as disparaging. He says that he didn't mean to belittle but was simply trying for contrast and is willing to drop it.

. . . those that gave you two answers to choose between . . .
(18)

This statement may not be sufficiently limited because the respondent may think of a free-answer question that also comes down to only two possible answers as far as he can see. The idea to make clear is that the two-way question itself *mentions* the two possibilities. So try again.

. . . those that STATED two answers to choose between . . . (19)

Notice that S. P. also dropped the "you," which is very clearly implied anyway.

As long as we are worshippers of the fetish of brevity, we might as well take every means of saving words that we can, so how about combining the "that stated" into "stating"?

. . . those STATING two answers to choose between . . .
(20)

S. P. may think I am being picayune, but there is one little thing about that word "choose." It missed being on the list of words in Chapter 9 because the Lorge magazine count placed it in the second thousand words by order of frequency. I would not say a thing about it except that so far all the rest of the words are on our frequent-familiar list and an adequate substitute for it happens to be there for the taking:

. . . those stating two answers to DECIDE between . . .
(21)

Maybe it's a point of honor with me, but I really would like to show you that a thousand words are enough for our needs even on a tough question like this. I think that now we can go on to the multiple-choice or cafeteria question alternative. I hope that S. P. will capitalize on what he has already learned from our struggle with the two-way question.

. . . THOSE STATING FOUR OR FIVE ANSWERS TO DECIDE AMONG . . .
(22)

Yes, sir! He is being downright slavish in following precedent. Still, the idea of deciding should carry over from the first alternative, so that he should be able to drop the last three words leaving:

. . . those stating four or five answers . . .
(23)

No one has ever restricted the meaning of "multiple-choice" to "four or five" answers before, at least not to my knowledge. Perhaps S. P. will accept this suggestion:

. . . those stating THREE OR MORE answers . . . (24)

Have you been noticing the prime example of "or" as a problem word in the last three versions? It may make this one alternative sound like two for those people who try to decide whether to take three *or* more answers. Fortunately, there is an easy way out of this problem.

. . . those stating MORE THAN TWO answers . . . (25)

So far, so good. S. P. moves on to the simplest, and therefore the hardest, idea of all to express—the free-answer question.

*. . . THOSE NOT STATING ANY ANSWERS BUT
WHERE YOU MADE UP THE ANSWERS YOUR-
SELF?* (26)

That seems to be a correct enough statement, but it is awfully long. We should be able to get along without that first clause.

. . . those where you made up the answers yourself? (27)

I can anticipate that our unimaginative respondent might bridle at this. I can hear him saying, "Do you suggest that I would *make up* an answer? I'll have you know that I'm absolutely honest!" How about getting S. P. to make another try?

*. . . THOSE THAT YOU ANSWERED IN YOUR
OWN WORDS?* (28)

Prestige rears its ugly head! Of course a person can state his ideas better in his own words than in the words of someone else! The same would go for this next version, too.

. . . those that you answered in your own WAY? (29)

The fault with these wordings is probably in the "your own" term, which plays up the respondent's individuality. S. P. says that it is easy enough to fix that.

*. . . THOSE WHERE YOU HAD TO THINK OF
AN ANSWER?* (30)

His loading here is in the other direction, and I for one would say that it is almost justified. People do have to struggle more to answer open questions than to answer the other types where the answers are placed before them. Perhaps they need to be reminded of this difficulty. But, who am I to say that this kind of loading is correct? How about another tack?

. . . those where you PROVIDED THE answer? (31)

No, we're sorry, but it won't do. The respondent "provides" the answer to every question. The same goes for the word "supply," so don't waste time in that direction.

. . . those where you GAVE WHATEVER ANSWER YOU WANTED? (32)

The same trouble! Respondents give whatever answers they want to two-way and multiple-choice questions, too.

. . . those where you gave AN ORIGINAL ANSWER? (33)

Whoops! He has slipped back into prestige again! Who doesn't want to be original? S. P. had better start over again.

. . . those where you gave ANY ANSWER YOU THOUGHT OF? (34)

That sounds harum-scarum, as though the respondent is expected to say the first thing that comes to mind.

. . . those where THERE WAS NO LIMIT TO THE POSSIBLE ANSWERS? (35)

This wording is technically correct, but it is stated from our point of view, not from the respondent's. It will probably not conjure up the idea of a free-answer question in his mind at all. He individually may not see limitless possibilities of answers in a free-answer question, but possibly only the one answer he gives. It is when we take all respondents as a group that we obtain the infinity of replies.

. . . THOSE THAT LEFT THE MATTER ENTIRELY UP TO YOU? (36)

Maybe S. P. is getting a little closer, but the "matter" is most indefinite. How about a more precise version of this same approach:

. . . those that left the STATEMENT OF THE ANSWER entirely up to you? (37)

Rather wordy, but he's on the right track.

. . . those that left the ANSWER OPEN FOR YOU TO STATE? (38)

The "open" probably contributes little to understanding. We can drop that one word and another by sacrificing the "that."

. . . those LEAVING the answer for you to state? (39)

Now I am reasonably well satisfied if you are, and I'm sure that S. P. will be glad to get it over with—so let's put it all together. That means the four parts from versions 13 21, 25, and 39.

Which questions did you like best—those stating two answers to decide between, those stating more than two answers, or those leaving the answer for you to state? (40)

Let's see. We wanted to compare this with our precise version, number 5, did we not?

Which do you prefer to be asked in opinion surveys—dichotomous, multiple-choice, or open questions? (5)

It looks to me as though we have managed to stay pretty close to the issue. The only difference, and I consider it a great improvement, is that our version now is based on immediate past experience and not on a hypothetical situation.

Before we try out this wording on respondents, we might well see how it compares with our list of frequent-familiar words in Chapter 9. When checked against that list, it looks like this:

√ √ † * *† * * † √
Which questions did you like best—those stating two
√ † √ √ * † * √ √
answers to decide between, those stating more than two
√ * * † * √ † * † †
answers, or those leaving the answer for you to state? (41)

Remarkable! Every single word is on the list, as indicated by a check mark or other symbol. So, you see, it is possible to get fairly complicated ideas down into familiar words.

The indicated problem words—you, like, best, those, more, or, and the—are not problems in the contexts used here. "You" clearly means the second person singular, not collective. "Like" does not introduce an example. "Best" is not used in the dead giveaway sense. The antecedent of "those" should be clear. The basis of comparison with "more" is stated. The "or" is used only to connect alternatives. "The" has no special overtones here.

None of the multi-meaning words is likely to be misunderstood in the present context.

The Flesch score would place this question in the readability range of eighth grade or high school students (32). The Dale-Chall score, on the other hand, would place it at the fifth grade level (38). The difference in these scores serves to emphasize how hazy the whole subject of readability is. At the same time, the direction the scores take shows us how difficult it is to achieve low-level readability. We have done about everything we can in stating the issue clearly and concisely, but we end up with 28 words as compared with 8 words in the original version.

Our next step is to outline what we want our interviewers to be on the lookout for in the pretesting.

First, have we succeeded in making this issue meaningful to respondents? That is, do they really know what we are talking about when we refer to the differences in the questions they have just been answering, or does it come as a sudden revelation to them that there could be different kinds of questions? If the latter is the case, then it means that we should carry S. P.'s idea a step farther. We could, for example, introduce every one of the preceding questions on our questionnaire in some such fashion as this:

(A) *Here is a question that states two answers for you to decide between: Which side of bed do you usually get out of—left or right?*

(B) *This one states more than two answers: Do you prefer to get up at five a.m., before five, or after five?*

(C) *On this next one, the answer is left for you to state: What do you like best about your alarm clock?*

By the time respondents have answered 15 or 20 questions with preambles of this sort, they should be conscious of the differences in types of questions, and our issue should by then be meaningful to them. This approach may sound ridiculously involved as a way of getting replies on just a single issue, but it does indicate the great lengths to which we may sometimes have to go to establish a common ground between questioner and respondent. When I tell you that on some subjects special pamphlets have been prepared for respondents to read before certain issues could be posed to them, perhaps this idea will not seem so outlandish to you.

Second, we should try to learn the frames of reference in which people answer this question. Do they think of particular questions instead of types of questions? If so, perhaps we should try a wording in terms of *Which KIND OF questions*. . . . We are gambling now that the "kind of" is an unneeded refinement, but we may be wrong. Do respondents tend to answer in terms of specific examples, such as "that one about my age" or "the one on my suggestions"? If so, we should try to find some way of steering them toward a more general course.

Third, what about the third alternative in particular? Does it actually bring to the respondent's mind what we intend it to, or does he think that the answers to all of our questions are left for him to state? And do the comments about it bring forth any evidence of the influence of prestige? The statement of this free-answer alternative has provided us an excellent illustration of the ever-present problem of loading. S. P. loaded it first one way and then another. The present version appears to fall somewhere in the middle, but is it loaded realistically? You remember that I almost favored loading it in this form—*questions where you have to think of an answer?*—because I happen to believe that the free-answer question does require more thought than the others do.

The approach we have adopted may enable us to obtain a rough idea of the prestige element here. If we should find in the pretest that a number of people who say they prefer the free-answer alternative have trouble with the actual free-answer questions they had been asked earlier in the questionnaire—if they fumble for words, habitually say they "don't know" to such questions, or give other evidence of not being at ease with free-answer questions—then we can say that their choice does not agree with their behavior. In such cases, the tester might even use the confrontation technique to ask them why they appear not to like such questions but end up saying they prefer them. This could be a very revealing experiment.

Fourth, is there any tendency for respondents to jump the gun on this question? I would not expect that to be the case, simply because I think that they will require a moment or so to comprehend it. But it does have some pauses indicated, so that our testers might as well be on the alert for anticipated replies.

Finally, if the question does come through the pretest satisfactorily, it would be highly advisable in the full-scale survey to use a split-ballot technique. With such a long question, it is of more than ordinary importance that each version be given an equal break:

Which questions did you like best—those stating two answers to decide between, those stating more than two answers, or those leaving the answer for you to state?

Which questions did you like best—those leaving the answer for you to state, those stating two answers to decide between, or those stating more than two answers?

Which questions did you like best—those stating more than two answers to decide among, those leaving the answer for you to state, or those stating two answers?

If right now or during the pretesting someone should shoot the question full of holes, that is just our bad luck and let's not hold S. P. responsible for it. It would mean that I would have been wiser to skip this thirteenth chapter just as a hotel builder skips the thirteenth floor.

14. How's that again?

NOBODY wants to read through a book, even as small a book as this, every time he words a question. Yet, any one of the many factors we have considered here may be enough to make the difference between a useful question and one which is misleading.

In this final chapter, therefore, I attempt to enumerate at least the most important features of question wording. A quick scanning of the items will help you make certain that every one of the features that applies has been given consideration in your questions. You can figuratively check them off one by one for each question until they become deeply ingrained in your thinking.

Actually you won't need this check list type of stimulus for long because most of these things are only common sense anyway. Having once been pointed out, they should stay with you pretty well with perhaps only an occasional reading for a refresher.

A. THE ISSUE

1. Make sure that you have a *clear understanding* of the issue *yourself*. This is of first importance if you are to make it meaningful to others.

2. See that the issue is *fully defined*. Check it for the Who? Why? When? Where? and How?

3. State the issue as *precisely* as you can at first. If in later versions you elect to sacrifice some precision, then at least the sacrifice will be recognized.

4. Attempt to evaluate whether the issue is *meaningful* to your *public*. If in your judgment it is not likely

to be meaningful to them, see whether you can find some way of increasing its penetrating power.

5. If you have reason to suspect that the issue still is not *sufficiently well known* to all parts of your public, give consideration to ways of segregating or eliminating the uninformed.

6. Try to assess the *stage of development* of the issue. It may be a mistake to ask a categorical question if opinion is still unformed and hazy on the subject. Conversely, if opinion is well crystallized or falls into definite patterns, the open question may be a waste of time.

7. Decide which *type of question* best fits the issue—free-answer, two-way, or multiple-choice—according to the preceding considerations.

8. Keep asking yourself, *"What am I taking for granted?"*

B. THE FREE-ANSWER QUESTION

9. Is it *necessary to ask this free-answer question* in the full-scale survey? Perhaps enough answers to it can be obtained in the pretest or in a subsample to serve the needs of the research. Remember that the coding of thousands of verbatim replies adds up to a lot of work!

10. Consider whether it is *convertible* to a categorical type of question. If the different points of view on the issue are generally well known, then you may wish to present them as alternatives (multiple-choice) rather than leave them to the respondents to articulate in their various ways.

11. Make it *sufficiently directive*. A free-answer question can be too broad and leave respondents as free as the birds to give answers from every direction and in every dimension. By carefully establishing the course, how-

ever, you can confine the answers to a particular frame of reference.

12. Indicate the *number of ideas* you expect from each respondent. If you accept one idea from this person and five ideas from that person, you don't know whether you are weighting respondents according to their articulateness or their weakness of conviction.

13. If you wish to extract all the thoughts you can on the subject, it may be advisable to add a *probe*.

14. Even though the question is in free-answer form, you may be able to provide *precoded* check boxes for the answers. This is especially likely if you are asking for amounts or figures.

C. TWO-WAY QUESTIONS

15. Avoid *implied alternatives*. No fault can be found with stating the alternative while some harm may result from leaving it to be carried by implication.

16. State the *negative in detail* where necessary. The "or not" may not be enough to give the negative side a fair shake.

17. In the *argument type* of two-way question it may be better to state both sides of the argument so that the respondent knows both the pro and the con.

18. "*Don't know*" or "*No opinion*" answers have to be provided for except in rare instances.

19. Consider whether there is a reasonable *middle-ground* position which some respondents might take. If so, you must then decide whether to state it for all respondents or not.

20. Ordinarily the choices should be *mutually exclusive*. If they cannot be made so, then you should add an answer box for the "Both" category and perhaps include the combination idea in the question itself.

21. The problem with *qualified answers* is a little differ-

ent. Your decision lies between providing a separate answer box for the qualified answers or not providing a separate box, thus forcing respondents into other categories.

22. If you anticipate a *variety of qualified answers*, it may be advisable to set up separate answer boxes for each variety.

23. The alternatives should be *complementary*. In some cases, however, it is wise to take account of the realities of the situation rather than use the literal opposites as complementary.

24. *All the alternatives* should be included. Remember our discussion of merit and seniority and other possible factors in promotions.

25. Give consideration to the *mildness* or *harshness* of the alternatives. The stronger the feeling implied by the alternatives, the fewer the choices that will be made.

26. Try to avoid the *unintended double-choice* type of question. Remember the "better-worse; now-then" example.

27. Many two-way questions are easily converted to the *fold-over* type in which you obtain both the expression of opinion and its intensity, in case you are interested in both.

D. MULTIPLE-CHOICE QUESTIONS

28. The choices need to be *mutually exclusive* in the multiple-choice question even more than in the two-way question.

29. *None of the alternatives* should be *overlooked* if a true expression of choices is desired. If combinations of the alternatives are possible, as in the royalties example, those combinations should be included.

30. It is all right to *restrict the choices*, however, if you keep this restriction in mind when interpreting the

results or actually state the restriction in the question. The example given earlier was in terms of "Aside from price, what . . .?"

31. The *number of alternatives* need not always be limited to only five or six as some people think.

32. The choices should be *well balanced* within a realistic framework. The number of alternatives presented on one side or another does affect the distribution of replies.

33. The issue should be *clear within each choice* in the degree-type question. That is, if war is mentioned in one alternative, it should not be left to implication in another.

34. Decide whether you want respondents to express *one choice* or *more than one* and then indicate your decision clearly for them.

35. You should give respondents a *card list* if the question has more than three alternatives.

36. Provide for *"Don't know"* or *"No opinion"* answers on the questionnaire, although you need not show them on the card list.

37. *Idea* alternatives may be stated in *varied orders* on different cards without affecting the order of the check boxes on the questionnaire.

38. *Numbers* should be listed in logical order out of courtesy.

39. Placing the *correct numbers* in a knowledge question at the *extremes* of the list is a wise move because respondents tend to guess the middle or average ones.

E. OTHER TYPES OF QUESTIONS

40. The *sleeper* question is useful in giving some clue to the amount of guesswork and irresponsible testimony in respondents' answers, but it has to be carefully constructed.

41. The *cheater* question is a means of catching the un-wary interviewer who fabricates his interviews, but it is not highly recommended.

42. *Single-purpose intensity* questions may be used after free-answer, two-way, or multiple-choice questions. They have wider application, therefore, than the fold-over type mentioned.

43. *Double-barreled* questions deserve to be split into separate questions for each of the two issues except in special cases where two issues necessarily have to be asked about together.

44. *Symbolized numbers* may help people to grasp box-car figures which otherwise might be outside their comprehension.

45. The *"or what?"* tag end is useful in some circum-stances, but it does not give the same results as would either a free-answer or multiple-choice question.

46. *Successive eliminators* are treacherous unless applied equally to each side of the original issue.

47. *Serialized* questions save time and irritation in cases where the same introduction and same alternatives apply to a number of questions.

48. Answers to a *which-is-the-whatest* question can best be evaluated in terms of the relative importance of the competing companies, products, or brands.

49. The *quintamensional design* reminds us of five ele-ments in an opinion—awareness, general opinion, spe-cific opinion, reasons, and intensity.

F. TREATMENT OF RESPONDENTS

50. Avoid the appearance of *talking down* or otherwise insulting the intelligence of your respondents.

51. Word your question according to principles of *good grammar* but don't make it sound stilted.

52. Don't sling *slang*.

[233]

53. And don't try to be *folksy*.

54. Beware the *double entendre* and shun the triple. "Please check your sex," for example, has three meanings—mark, restrain, and verify.

55. Skip the *salesmanship*—unless you are doing research on a sales approach.

56. Do what you can to help your respondents, not to *confuse* them.

57. When it comes to seemingly inconsistent replies, however, you may discover something by *confronting* respondents with their apparent inconsistencies.

58. *Double negatives* should not be inflicted on anyone.

59. *Tricky* questions can be tricky indeed. Don't be tricked by them yourself.

60. If there can be any possible question about the *antecedent*, restate it.

61. Keep away from wordings that beg for *ambiguous answers*. A "Yes" that means "No" is worse than a "Don't know."

62. A difficult problem is to make your question *specific* enough without making it over-elaborate.

63. Remember that your *fine distinctions* will often not be understood by the respondents.

64. To avoid unnecessary quibbling on the part of some respondents, it may be necessary to provide a *peg* on which they can hang their ideas.

G. THE WORDS THEMSELVES

65. Use as *few words as necessary*. You can ask most questions in twenty words or less.

66. Use *simple words* if you can find any that adequately express the idea.

67. When you use a *polysyllabic* word, put a ring around it so the tester will know that it is especially suspect.

68. *Trade jargon* may be all right to use in the trade, if

all the trade uses it, but it will not do for the general public.

69. Check in the dictionary to see if the word actually does have the *meaning* you intend.

70. While there, see what *other meanings* it may have which could confuse the issue.

71. Make sure the word has only one *pronunciation*.

72. Look into the possibility of *homonyms*, as in the case of the boy with the stomachache who told the hospital attendant his address was "eight-one-two Greene."

73. If you use a *synonym*, make sure that it actually is synonymous with the idea at hand.

74. Avoid *concept* words. In fact, you may be wise not to attempt to explore concept issues.

75. Words that are *frequently used* are to be preferred, other things being equal, of course.

76. *Familiar words* are the most useful if they don't have too many meanings in context.

77. The *problem words* may or may not be problems, depending on the context.

H. LOADING

78. It is on *marginal issues*, which the public knows little about and cares little about, that loading can most easily distort the picture of public opinion.

79. Citing the *status quo* introduces a powerful influence beyond the merits of the issue.

80. Among the possible *prestige* influences to be eliminated or counter-balanced are appeals to one's wisdom, knowledge, fairness, affluence, physical attributes, morals, and devotion to duty.

81. Expressions of *wishful thinking* need to be exposed for what they are rather than taken as predictions of future action.

82. Unless a *stereotype* is itself an important part of the

issue, you will want to avoid using it when obtaining evaluations of the issue.

83. The *dead giveaway* is always bad.

84. Be alert to the difference between *means and ends*.

85. Surrounding *circumstances* may affect the answers unless you find means of counteracting them.

86. The *well-known* may have an advantage over the little-known so that it may be necessary for you to make a complete introduction of both.

87. A *personalized* question may produce different answers than an impersonalized one.

88. Answers to *hypothetical* questions may not be so valid in predictions of future behavior as answers in terms of past experiences may be.

89. You may find it necessary to establish some kind of *standards of comparison* for respondents to use.

90. *Extensive* questions should not attempt to cover more territory than the respondents can readily comprehend.

91. Introduction of *examples* may divert attention from the issue to the examples.

I. READABILITY

92. *Misplaced emphasis* can be minimized by underscoring the words which should be emphasized.

93. *Gun jumping* on the part of respondents can be reduced by holding back the alternatives until the conditions have been stated.

94. Eliminate *unnecessary punctuation* because a pause may be taken as the end of the question.

95. Indicate *correct pronunciation* of difficult words.

96. Be wary of using *homographs* such as "lead" and "lead."

97. *Tongue twisters* have no place in survey questions.

98. Spell out all *abbreviations* as you want interviewers to say them.

99. Instead of the indefinite *"how much?"* approach, you can save work for yourself by indicating the system in which you want the answers to come—percentages, dollars, miles, pints, or whatever.

100. For possible *trend* purposes, try to imagine how the question will sound five years hence and adjust it to fit that possibility.

One last recommendation that I have already stated many times but which deserves the prominence of these final words is this: Controlled experiment is the surest way of making progress in our understanding of question wording. Never overlook an opportunity to employ the *split-ballot* technique.

Thank you!

References

(1) Robinson, C. E., *Straw Votes*, Columbia University Press, 1932.
(2) *The Pre-Election Polls of 1948*, Social Science Research Council, 1949.
(3) Hovde, Howard T. "Recent Trends in the Development of Market Research," *American Marketing Journal*, 1936, No. 3, p. 3.
(4) Stouffer, S. A., *et al.*, *Measurement and Prediction*, Vol. IV in Studies in Social Psychology in World War II, sponsored by the Social Science Research Council. Princeton University Press, 1950, p. 709.
(5) Katz, Daniel, "Survey Techniques and Polling Procedures as Methods in Social Science," *Journal of Social Issues*, 1946.
(6) Blankenship, Albert B., *Consumer and Opinion Research*, Harper and Brothers, 1943.
(7) *Urban Enumerators Reference Manual*, U.S. Bureau of the Census, Washington, D.C.
(8) Bancroft, Gertrude, and Welch, Emmett H., "Recent Experience with Problems of Labor Force Measurement," *Journal of the American Statistical Association*, September 1946, p. 303.
(9) "Summary Statement for the 1942 Dwelling Unit Occupancy Surveys," U.S. Bureau of the Census, March 1943.
(10) Gill, Sam, "How Do You Stand on Sin?" *Tide* magazine, March 14, 1947, pp. 72ff.
(11) American Institute of Public Opinion news service release, February 12, 1947; March 11, 1949; March 23, 1949; May 1, 1949.
(12) Kitt, Alice S., and Gleicher, David B., "Determinants of Voting Behavior," *Public Opinion Quarterly*, Fall 1950, p. 393.
(13) "The Public's Appraisal of Banks and Banking," Association of Reserve City Bankers, 1947.
(14) "Do Polls Accurately Reflect Opinion?" *Railway Age*, March 30, 1946.
(15) "Experience in the *Time* International Survey—The Universe, Translation and Timing," *Public Opinion Quarterly*, Winter 1948, pp. 713-714.
(16) Gallup, George, "The Quintamensional Plan of Question Design," *Public Opinion Quarterly*, Fall 1947, p. 385.
(17) Cantril, Hadley, and Rugg, Donald, *Gauging Public Opinion*, Princeton University Press, 1944, Chapter II.

(18) Lazarsfeld, Paul F., "The Art of Asking Why," *National Marketing Review*, 1935, Vol. I, No. 1.

(19) Hyman, Herbert, and Stember, Herbert, "Interviewer Effects in the Classification of Responses," *Public Opinion Quarterly*, Winter 1949, pp. 669-682.

(20) "Wording and Order of Questions," Minutes of Panel 8 of the 1946 Central City Conference on Public Opinion Research, published by the National Opinion Research Center, University of Denver.

(21) Zeisel, Hans, *Say It With Figures*, Harper and Brothers, 1947.

(22) Rugg, Donald, "Experiments in Wording Questions: II," *Public Opinion Quarterly*, Vol. 5, No. 1, March 1941.

(23) Cantril, Hadley, and Fried, Edrita, *Gauging Public Opinion*, Princeton University Press, 1944, Chapter I.

(24) Guttman, Louis, and Suchman, Edward A., "Intensity and a Zero Point for Attitude Analysis," *American Sociological Review*, February 1947, pp. 57, 67.

(25) Robinson, Claude, "The Strange Case of the Taft-Hartley Law," *Look* magazine, September 30, 1947, p. 68.

(26) Barlow, Walter G., and Payne, Stanley L., "A Tool for Evaluating Company Community Relations," *Public Opinion Quarterly*, Fall 1949, p. 405.

(27) Berrey, Lester V., and Van den Bark, Melvin, *The American Thesaurus of Slang*, Thomas Y. Crowell, 1942.

(28) Wembridge, E. R., and Means, E. R., "Voting on the Double Negative," *Journal of Applied Psychology*, 1918, No. 2, pp. 156-163.

(29) A report by Opinion Research Corporation, *Those Who Know You Well . . . Think Well of You*, American Petroleum Institute, November 1946.

(30) Wheeler, Elmer, *Tested Sentences That Sell*, Prentice-Hall Company, 1938.

(31) Payne, Stanley L., "Case Study in Question Complexity," *Public Opinion Quarterly*, Winter 1949-50, p. 653.

(32) Flesch, Rudolf, *The Art of Plain Talk*, Harper and Brothers, 1946.

(33) Terris, Fay, "Are Poll Questions Too Difficult?" *Public Opinion Quarterly*, Summer 1949, pp. 314-319.

(34) Richards, I. A., *Basic English and Its Uses*, W. W. Norton and Co., 1943.

(35) Chase, Stuart, *The Proper Study of Mankind*, Harper and Brothers, 1948.

(36) Thorndike, E. L. *Thorndike Century Senior Dictionary*, Scott, Foresman and Co., 1941.

(37) Thorndike, E. L., and Lorge, Irving, *The Teacher's Word Book of 30,000 Words*, Columbia University, 1944.

(38) Dale, Edgar, and Chall, Jeanne S., *A Formula for Predicting Readability*, Ohio State University, Educational Research Bulletin, 1948, Vol. 27, pp. 11-20, 37-54.

(39) Chase, Stuart, *The Tyranny of Words*, Harcourt, Brace and Company, 1938.

(40) Crespi, Leo P., "The Interview Effect in Polling," *Public Opinion Quarterly*, Spring 1948, pp. 99-111.

(41) Kornhauser, Arthur, "Are Public Opinion Polls Fair to Organized Labor?" *Public Opinion Quarterly*, Winter 1946, pp. 484-500.

(42) Link, Henry C., *et al.*, "Is Dr. Kornhauser Fair to Organized Pollers?" *Public Opinion Quarterly*, Summer 1947, pp. 198-204.

(43) Parry, Hugh J., and Crossley, Helen M., "Validity of Responses to Survey Questions," *Public Opinion Quarterly*, Spring 1950, pp. 61-80.

(44) Kinsey, Alfred C.; Pomeroy, Wardell B.; Martin, Clyde E., *Sexual Behavior in the Human Male*, Chapter II, W. B. Saunders Company, 1948.

(45) Riesman, David, and Glazer, Nathan, "The Meaning of Opinion," *Public Opinion Quarterly*, Winter 1948-49, p. 633.

(46) Bulletins No. 636-649, U.S. Dept. of Labor, Bureau of Labor Statistics.

(47) Menefee, Selden C., "The Effect of Stereotyped Words on Political Judgments," *American Sociological Review*, Vol. I, pp. 614-621.

(48) Payne, Stanley L., "Some Opinion Research Principles Developed through Studies of Socialized Medicine," *Public Opinion Quarterly*, Spring 1946, p. 93.

(49) Dollard, John, "Under What Conditions Do Opinions Predict Behavior?" *Public Opinion Quarterly*, Winter 1948, pp. 628-632.

(50) Gallup, George, and Rae, Saul Forbes, *The Pulse of Democracy*, Simon and Schuster, 1940.

(51) Hubbard, Alfred W., "Phrasing Questions," *Journal of Marketing*, July 1950, p. 48.

(52) *U.S.* v. *88 Cases (Bireley's Orange Beverage)*, Civil Action No. 4711 (1945) (U.S. D.C. N.J.).

(53) Deming, W. Edwards, *Some Theory of Sampling*, John Wiley & Sons, 1950.

General Index

[244]

aways, 183, 192f, 236; experimental, 182; hypothetical questions, 198f, 213, 218, 236; known vs. unknown, 196, 236; means vs. ends, 193f, 236; one-sided, 177, 182f, 222f; personalization, 196ff, 236; prestige, 184-189, 226, 235; status quo, 183f, 235; stereotypes, 189ff, 235f; suggestibility, 178f; see also: predispositions
loose vs. tight questions, 131-137, 207
Lorge, Irving, 143, 241

mail questionnaires, 7, 13, 18f, 59
Martin, Clyde E., 186, 241
Means, E. R., 124, 240
Menefee, Selden C., 190, 241
middle-ground words, 141-147
Monthly Report on Labor Force, 11
multi-meaning (ambiguous) words, 22, 53f, 138f, 142f, 145, 147, 150, 175, 225, 235; in word list, 151-157
multiple answers, 51, 54, 88f, 230, 232
multiple-choice (cafeteria) questions, 75-99, 231ff; alternatives, number of, 92ff, 232; balance, 90ff, 232; card lists, 78-91, 93-96, 98, 232; compared with other types, 32f, 49f, 74-78, 82, 92, 95f, 98ff, 105f, 229, 233; degree (gradation) questions, 32, 75, 94-98, 232; in demonstration of wording, 215-219, 221, 224-227; fold-over questions, 97f, 102, 231; formality of, 75f; idea type, 84-88, 232; knowledge (awareness) questions, 79-84, 179; multiple answers, 88f, 232; number lists, 80-84, 232; in quintamensional design, 112; variety questions, 32, 75-94

name as part of issue, 191f
National Better Business Bureau, 173
National Housing Agency, 11
negatives, mild wordings for, 24, 162
numbers, effects of lists, 80-84, 232; logical order, 86, 123, 232; symbolized, 104f, 200, 233

obvious, neglect of the, 3, 52
occupations, coding, 42f, 45; prestige, 185, 188

Office of Price Administration, 22
omnibus questions, 103f
Opinion Research Corporation, 8
opinion surveys, 7, 15, 202, 216, 218
opposite meanings of words, 22, 141f, 159, 212
or what? questions, 32, 105f, 233
outsmarting oneself, 125f
over-elaboration, 122, 234

Parry, Hugh J., 185, 241
past preference build-up, 186, 189
past tense (experience) questions, 199, 218f, 236
Payne, Stanley L., 110, 129, 193, 196, 240, 241
pegs for ideas, 127, 234
personalized questions, 39, 196ff, 236
Pomeroy, Wardell B., 186, 241
positive vs. negative statement, 123f
pre-coding, 44-48, 56, 73, 183, 230
predispositions, against criticizing, 23f, 186; best-known alternative, 109ff; conformance, 70, 86; toward examples, 168, 173, 211, 219, 226, 236; first-seen alternative, 84, 134; last-heard alternative, 72, 133ff; middle-ground, moderation, 63ff, 81, 96; middle numbers, 80-84, 134, 232; normal answers, 198; toward having opinions, 18, 186f; toward pleasing answers, 72; political behavior, 24, 186, 189; prestige, 114, 184-189, 222, 226, 235; status quo, 167, 183f, 235; stereotypes, 189ff, 235f; wishful thinking, 187f, 235; see also: loaded questions
Pre-Election Polls of 1948, 4, 239
premature answers (gun-jumping), 134, 204-207, 227, 236
pre-testing, 6, 13-16, 23, 147, 149, 219, 225ff, 229, 234
problem words, 148, 150, 221, 224f, 235; listed, 151-157; discussed, 158-176
pronunciation difficulties, 141f, 203, 208f, 235f
propagandistic questions, 103, 178
Public Opinion Index for Industry, 8
Public Opinion Quarterly, 110, 129, 193f, 239ff
punctuation, 134, 203, 207f, 236
punsters, function of, 120

qualified answers, 60ff, 230f
question types, different results by, 76ff; pros and cons of, 32f, 49-55, 69f, 74-79, 82, 92, 95f, 98ff, 105f, 229, 233
quibbling, 66, 103, 120, 160, 234
quintamensional design, 32, 112f, 187, 233

Rae, Saul Forbes, 206, 241
Railway Age, 26, 239
readability scores, 124, 136f, 225
recall different from fact, 29
reenforcing replies, 52
respondents, articulateness of, 36, 52, 230; misspeaking, 69, 79; motives, 17, 114, 184f
Richards, I. A., 139, 240
Riesman, David, 186, 241
Robinson, Claude E., 4, 104, 239f
Ruch, Floyd L., 48
Rugg, W. Donald, xii, 33, 57, 63, 65, 91, 196f, 239f

sampling, 4f, 9, 14, 177, 215
scale and intensity analysis, 97
selling ideas, 115, 128, 234
serialized questions, 108f, 233
simple words, need for, 129-137, 234; misleading, 27f; clumsy circumlocution, 149
single-meaning words, 138f, 141-144
slang, 54, 119, 164ff, 168, 172, 174, 233
sleeper questions, 100f, 232
Social Science Research Council, 4, 239
space, effect on answers, 51
specificity, 37f, 48f, 121f, 143, 176, 234
split-ballot technique, 73f, 84ff, 129, 182, 184, 192, 197, 207, 227, 237
stability not a test, 17
standards for comparison, 104f, 200, 233, 236
Stember, Herbert, 45, 240
Stephan, Frederick F., 5
sterile opinion, 191f
Stern, Eric, 28
Stouffer, Samuel A., 5, 239
strength of opinion, 58, 61, 64, 135, 179f
Study of Consumer Income, 188, 201, 241
successive eliminator questions, 106f, 233

Suchman, Edward A., 97, 240
synonyms, 8, 116, 163, 168, 173, 235
suggestible questions, 49, 178

talking down, 115ff, 233
Teacher's Word Book, 143, 241
Terris, Fay, 137, 240
Tested Sentences That Sell, 128, 240
thesaurus, use of, 141
Thorndike Century Senior Dictionary, 150f, 240
Thorndike, E. L., 143, 240f
three-syllable (or more) words, 66, 136, 149, 234
trend questions, 212f, 237
trick questions, 17f, 115, 234
two-way (dichotomous) questions, 55-74, 230f; described, 54f; additional alternatives, 59-64, 70f, 231; argument questions, 71f, 230; compared with other types, 32f, 49f, 69f, 74-78, 92, 95f, 98ff, 105f, 229, 233; in demonstration of wording, 17f, 20, 214-221, 224-227; precoding, 56, 73; probing, 59; qualified answers, 60ff, 230f; in quintamensional design, 112; verbatim answers, 62; see also: alternatives
Tyranny of Words, 149, 241

unaided recall, 40
unfamiliar terms, 12f, 18, 66, 140, 146f, 214, 217
uninformed, eliminating the, 40, 229
units indicated, 46

Van den Bark, Melvin, 119, 165, 240

Welch, Emmett H., 11, 239
Wembridge, E. R., 124, 240
Wheeler, Elmer, 128, 240
which-is-the-whatest questions, 109ff, 233
Who? Why? When? Where? How?, 26f, 216, 228
word count, 143ff, 147ff, 158, 221
word list, 151-157
wording not a game, 9, 15
written vs. oral communication, 136f, 146

Zeisel, Hans, 48, 59, 240

Index of Examples

[247]